INTRODUCTION TO FIRST EDITION

Civil War Commanders presents a photographic image and capsule biography of over one hundred Union and Confederate officers. The book is by no means intended to replace the valuable reference works *Generals in Gray* and *Generals in Blue* by Ezra J. Warner, or *The Civil War Dictionary* by Mark M. Boatner III. Rather, it is the intention to highlight the careers of a few individuals and illustrate many views of them not commonly encountered. The selection process was at times difficult and the number of commanders has grown since the original list, but a stopping point had to be reached. It is felt, however, that an equitable number of Confederate and Union commanders from across the United States have been included.

Each concise biography is in the same format. The following information will be found for every commander: date of birth; place of birth; attendance at the U.S. Military Academy, West Point, New York, including class year, position and size of class (X/X), branch of service to which graduate was posted; pre-war experience; rank(s) during the Civil War; major battles and campaigns (troops commanded); post-war achievements; date of death; and place of burial.

All photographs, unless otherwise indicated, are courtesy of the U.S. Army Military History Institute and are to be found in the collection of the Massachusetts Commandery of the Military Order of the Loyal Legion of the United States. The publisher is indebted to Mr. Michael J. Winey and Mr. Randy W. Hackenburg for their assistance. In addition, thanks are due the following for their important contributions: Mr. Stephen V. Ash, Mr. Daniel W. Brown – Fort Pulaski National Monument, Mr. Joe Hertel, Mr. Wendell W. Lang, Jr. – Library of Congress, Mr. Alan Sessarego, Mr. Karl Sundstrom, and Mr. Bill Turner.

If this work causes the reader to further his or her interest or knowledge of Civil War history – it will have served its purpose.

Dean S. Thomas
Arendtsville, PA
March 1986

INTRODUCTION TO SECOND EDITION

The favorable response to the original *Civil War Commanders* has led to the decision to expand this work from 111 to 138 personalities. Even with suggestions and recommendations from numerous individuals, this revised edition probably still does not contain everyone's favorites; however, the new additions do present a wider geographical representation from both sides of the Mason-Dixon line. We offer our thanks to the Civil War Library and Museum, the Museum of the Confederacy, Mr. Bill Turner, and the U.S. Army Military History Institute for their assistance in providing the photographs.

Dean S. Thomas
Gettysburg, PA
July 1988

THE COMMANDERS

Alexander, Edward Porter
Anderson, Richard Heron
Anderson, Robert
Ashby, Turner
Banks, Nathaniel Prentiss
Beauregard, Pierre Gustave Toutant
Birney, David Bell
Bowen, John Stevens
Bragg, Braxton
Breckinridge, John Cabell
Buckner, Simon Bolivar
Buell, Don Carlos
Buford, John
Burnside, Ambrose Everett
Butler, Bemjamin Franklin
Chamberlain, Joshua Lawrence
Churchill, Thomas James
Cleburne, Patrick Ronayne
Crawford, Samuel Wylie
Crittenden, Thomas Leonidas
Curtis, Samuel Ryan
Custer, George Armstrong
Davis, Jefferson Columbus
Davis, Jefferson Finis
Doubleday, Abner
Early, Jubal Anderson
Ewell, Richard Stoddert
Farragut, David Glasgow
Floyd, John Buchanan
Forney, John Horace
Forrest, Nathan Bedford
Franklin, William Buel
Fremont, John Charles
Garfield, James Abram
Geary, John White
Gibbon, John
Gillmore, Quincy Adams
Gordon, John Brown
Granger, Gordon
Grant, Ulysses Simpson
Halleck, Henry Wager
Hampton, Wade
Hancock, Winfield Scott
Hardee, William Joseph
Harrison, Benjamin
Hayes, Rutherford Birchard

Heth, Henry
Hill, Ambrose Powell
Hill, Daniel Harvey
Hood, John Bell
Hooker, Joseph
Howard, Oliver Otis
Hunt, Henry Jackson
Hunter, David
Jackson, Thomas Jonathan
Johnson, Andrew
Johnson, Bushrod Rust
Johnson, Edward
Johnston, Albert Sidney
Johnston, Joseph Eggleston
Kershaw, Joseph Brevard
Kilpatrick, Hugh Judson
Lee, Fitzhugh
Lee, Robert Edward
Lee, Stephen Dill
Lincoln, Abraham
Logan, John Alexander
Longstreet, James
Loring, William Wing
Lyon, Nathaniel
Magruder, John Bankhead
Mahone, William
McClellan, George Brinton
McClernand, John Alexander
McCook, Alexander McDowell
McCullough, Ben
McDowell, Irvin
McKinley, William
McLaws, Lafayette
McPherson, James Birdseye
Meade, George Gordon
Miles, Dixon Stansbury
Morgan, George Washington
Morgan, John Hunt
Mosby, John Singleton
Olmstead, Charles Hart
Ord, Edward Otho Cresap
Palmer, John McCauley
Parke, John Grubb
Paxton, Elisha Franklin
Pegram, John
Pelham, John

Pemberton, John Clifford
Pender, William Dorsey
Pendleton, William Nelson
Pettigrew, James Johnston
Pickett, George Edward
Pike, Albert
Pillow, Gideon Johnson
Pleasonton, Alfred
Polk, Leonidas
Pope, John
Porter, David Dixon
Porter, Fitz John
Prentiss, Benjamin Mayberry
Price, Sterling
Ramseur, Stephen Dodson
Reynolds, John Fulton
Richardson, Isreal Bush
Ricketts, James Brewerton
Rodes, Robert Emmett
Rosecrans, William Starke
Rosser, Thomas Lafayette
Schofield, John McAllister
Scott, Winfield
Sedgwick, John
Sheridan, Philip Henry
Sherman, William Tecumseh
Sickles, Daniel Edgar
Slemmer, Adam Jacoby
Slocum, Henry Warner
Smith, Edmund Kirby
Smith, Martin Luther
Stevenson, Carter Littlepage
Stewart, Alexander Peter
Stuart, James Ewell Brown
Sumner, Edwin Vose
Sykes, George
Thomas, George Henry
Trimble, Isaac Ridgeway
Upton, Emory
VanDorn, Earl
Wallace, Lewis
Walker, William Henry Talbot
Warren, Gouverneur Kemble
Wheeler, Joseph
Wilson, James Harrison
Wirz, Henry Hartmann

Edward Porter Alexander

Confederate

Date of birth: May 26, 1835

Birthplace: Washington, Georgia

U.S. Military Academy: Class of 1857 (3/38) Artillery

Pre-war experience: Utah Expedition, instructor at West Point, resigned from U.S. Army on May 1, 1861

Rank: Captain of Engineers, Major, Lt. Colonel, Colonel, and Brig. General of Artillery

Major Battles and Campaigns: First Manassas, Seven Days, Second Manassas, Antietam, Fredericksburg, Chancellorsville, Chief of Artillery of Longstreet's Corps at Gettysburg, Chickamauga, Knoxville, Spotsylvania, Cold Harbor, Petersburg - wounded, defense of the James River, retreat to Appomattox

Post-war achievements: professor of engineering at S.C. University, railroad president, planter, author, held various public positions

Date of death: April 28, 1910

Place of burial: City Cemetery, Augusta, Georgia

Richard Heron Anderson

Confederate

Date of birth: October 7, 1821

Birthplace: Sumter County, South Carolina

U.S. Military Academy: Class of 1842 (40/56) Dragoons

Pre-war experience: Mexican War, Kansas border disputes, resigned from U.S. Army on March 3, 1861

Rank: Colonel - 1st S.C. Inf., Brig. General, Major General, Lt. General

Major Battles and Campaigns: Fort Sumter (1st S.C.); Peninsular Campaign (Brigade); Second Manassas, Antietam - wounded, Fredericksburg, Chancellorsville, Gettysburg, Wilderness (Division); Spotsylvania, Cold Harbor, Petersburg (commanded Longstreet's Corps); Richmond defenses, Sayler's Creek (Division)

Post-war achievements: financially unsuccessful

Date of death: June 26, 1879

Place of burial: Beaufort, South Carolina

Robert Anderson

Union

Date of birth: June 14, 1805

Birthplace: near Louisville, Kentucky

U.S. Military Academy: Class of 1825 (15/37) Artillery

Pre-war experience: Black Hawk, Seminole and Mexican Wars, instructor at West Point, commanded defenses of Charleston Harbor, S.C.

Rank: Major, Brig. General

Major Battles and Campaigns: Fort Sumter (commander); Department of Kentucky, Department of the Cumberland, retired in 1863

Post-war achievements: raised United States flag over Fort Sumter on April 14, 1865

Date of death: October 26, 1871

Place of burial: West Point, New York

Turner Ashby

Confederate

Date of birth: October 23, 1828

Birthplace: "Rose Bank," Fauquier County, Virginia

U.S. Military Academy: no

Pre-war experience: grain dealer, planter, politician, led a volunteer cavalry company to Harpers Ferry in 1859

Rank: Captain, Major, Lt. Colonel, Colonel - 7th Virginia Cavalry, Brig. General

Major Battles and Campaigns: Jackson's Shenandoah Valley Campaign (Brigade) - killed fighting rear guard action near Harrisonburg, VA (a legend in his own time)

Post-war achievements: none

Date of death: June 6, 1862

Place of burial: Stonewall Cemetery, Winchester, Virginia

Taken after his death, the only known photo of Ashby in the flesh.

Bill Turner

5

Nathaniel Prentiss Banks

Union

Date of birth: January 30, 1816

Birthplace: Waltham, Massachusetts

U.S. Military Academy: no

Pre-war experience: lawyer, Massachusetts legislator, U.S. House of Representatives (four terms) Speaker in 1856, Governor of Massachusetts 1858-1861

Rank: Major General

Major Battles and Campaigns: Kernstown - Jackson's Shenandoah Valley Campaign (V Corps); Cedar Mountain (II Corps); Red River Campaign of 1863, Port Hudson, Red River Campaign of 1864 (commander, Department of the Gulf)

Post-war achievements: U.S. House of Representatives (six terms), Massachusetts senate, U.S. marshal

Date of death: September 1, 1894

Place of burial: Grove Hill Cemetery, Waltham, Massachusetts

Pierre Gustave Toutant Beauregard

Confederate

Date of birth: May 28, 1818

Birthplace: Saint Bernard Parish, Louisiana

U.S. Military Academy: Class of 1838 (2/45) Engineers

Pre-war experience: Mexican War - wounded twice, engineering assignments, Superintendent of West Point for less than a week in January 1861, resigned from U.S. Army on February 20, 1861

Rank: Brig. General, Full General

Major Battles and Campaigns: Fort Sumter (commanded C.S. forces); First Manassas (commanded line); Shiloh (2nd in command to A.S. Johnston); defenses of the South Carolina and Georgia coasts - 1863; Drewry's Bluff; Petersburg; Carolinas Campaign - 1865 (2nd in command to J.E. Johnston)

Post-war achievements: railroad president, supervisor of the Louisiana Lottery, Adjutant General of Louisiana, writer

Date of death: February 20, 1893

Place of burial: Metairie Cemetery, New Orleans, Louisiana

David Bell Birney
Union

Date of birth: May 29, 1825

Birthplace: Huntsville, Alabama

U.S. Military Academy: no

Pre-war experience: Andover College, studied law in Cincinnati, Ohio; lawyer in Philadelphia, Pa.

Rank: Lt. Col. & Colonel - 23rd Pennsylvania, Brig. General, Major General

Major Battles and Campaigns: Peninsular Campaign, Seven Pines (Brigade - III Corps); Second Manassas; Chantilly (Brigade/Kearny's Division); Fredericksburg, Chancellorsville (Division - III Corps); Gettysburg - slightly wounded (Division/III Corps); Wilderness, Spotsylvania, Cold Harbor, (Division - II Corps); Petersburg, (II Corps, X Corps) - contracted malaria

Post-war achievements: none, died of natural causes

Date of death: October 18, 1864

Place of burial: Woodlands Cemetery, Philadelphia, Pennsylvania

John Stevens Bowen
Confederate

Date of birth: October 30, 1830

Birthplace: Savannah, Georgia

U.S. Military Academy: Class of 1853 (13/51) Mounted Rifles

Pre-war experience: Frontier duty before resigning in 1856, architect in Savannah and St. Louis

Rank: Capt. - Missouri militia, Colonel - 1st Missouri, Brig. General, Major General

Major Battles and Campaigns: captured at Camp Jackson, MO by Lyon; Shiloh – wounded (Brigade); Port Gibson, Vicksburg (Division)

Post-war achievements: none, died from dysentery a paroled prisoner

Date of death: July 13, 1863

Place of burial: Confederate Cemetery, Vicksburg, Mississippi

Eleanor S. Brockenbrough Library   Museum of the Confederacy

Braxton Bragg

Confederate

Date of birth: March 22, 1817

Birthplace: Warrenton, North Carolina

U.S. Military Academy: Class of 1837 (5/50) Artillery

Pre-war experience: Seminole and Mexican Wars, resigned from U.S. Army in 1856 and became a planter

Rank: Brig. General, Major General, Full General

Major Battles and Campaigns: Shiloh (Confederate Right); Perryville, Stones River, Tullahoma Campaign, Chickamauga, Chattanooga (commanded Army of Tennessee); military advisor to Jefferson Davis from February 1864

Post-war achievements: civil engineer

Date of death: September 27, 1876

Place of burial: Mobile, Alabama

John Cabell Breckinridge

Confederate

Date of birth: January 15, 1821

Birthplace: near Lexington, Kentucky

U.S. Military Academy: no

Pre-war experience: Centre College, Transylvania University, lawyer, U.S. House of Representatives, Vice-President of the United States under Buchanan, U.S. Senator

Rank: Brig. General, Major General

Major Battles and Campaigns: Shiloh (Reserve Corps); Baton Rouge; Stones River (Division, Hardee's Corps); Vicksburg Campaign, Chickamauga, Missionary Ridge (Division, D.H. Hill's Corps); Cold Harbor, Early's Raid - 1864 (Division); Confederate Secretary of War

Post-war achievements: lawyer

Date of death: May 17, 1875

Place of burial: Lexington, Kentucky

Simon Bolivar Buckner
Confederate

Date of birth: April 1, 1823

Birthplace: Hart County, Kentucky

U.S. Military Academy: Class of 1844 (11/25) Infantry

Pre-war experience: Mexican War, instructor at West Point, resigned from U.S. Army in 1855, businessman in Chicago, Adjutant General of Kentucky

Rank: Brig. General, Major General, Lt. General

Major Battles and Campaigns: Fort Donelson (commanded after Floyd and Pillow fled); Perryville (Division, Hardee's Corps); Chickamauga (Corps); Trans-Mississippi with E.K. Smith

Post-war achievements: newspaper editor, Governor of Kentucky 1887-1892, Vice-presidential nominee in 1896

Date of death: January 8, 1914

Place of burial: State Cemetery, Frankfurt, Kentucky

Don Carlos Buell
Union

Date of birth: March 23, 1818

Birthplace: Lowell, Ohio

U.S. Military Academy: Class of 1841 (32/52) Infantry

Pre-war experience: Seminole and Mexican Wars, line and staff assignments from Atlantic to Pacific coasts

Rank: Lt. Colonel, Brig. General, Major General

Major Battles and Campaigns: Shiloh, Corinth Campaign, Perryville (commanding General, Department of the Ohio; replaced by Rosecrans, May 1863 to June 1864 he was "waiting orders" in Indianapolis, resigned from U.S. Army on June 1, 1864

Post-war achievements: businessman, pension agent

Date of death: November 19, 1898

Place of burial: Bellefontaine Cemetery, St. Louis, Missouri

John Buford
Union

Date of birth: March 4, 1826

Birthplace: Woodford County, Kentucky

U.S. Military Academy: Class of 1848 (16/38) Dragoons-Cavalry

Pre-war experience: Utah Expedition, frontier duty

Rank: Major, Brig. General, Major General

Major Battles and Campaigns: Thoroughfare Gap (Brigade); Second Manassas - wounded; Chief of Cavalry in Antietam Campaign, Fredericksburg, Stoneman's Raid, Gettysburg Campaign, Gettysburg (Cavalry Division)

Post-war achievements: none, died of natural causes

Date of death: December 16, 1863

Place of burial: West Point, New York

Ambrose Everett Burnside
Union

Date of birth: May 23, 1824

Birthplace: Liberty, Union County, Indiana

U.S. Military Academy: Class of 1847 (18/38) Artillery

Pre-war experience: Mexican War, garrison duty, resigned from U.S. Army in 1853, arms inventor and manufacturer, Rhode Island militia General, railroad treasurer

Rank: Colonel - 1st Rhode Island, Brig. General, Major General

Major Battles and Campaigns: First Manassas (Brigade); led Expedition to North Carolina; Antietam (Corps); commander of the Army of the Potomac at Fredericksburg; Department of the Ohio, Knoxville; Wilderness, Spotsylvania, North Anna, Petersburg "Crater" (IX Corps)

Post-war achievements: businessman, Governor of Rhode Island, U.S. Senator

Date of death: September 13, 1881

Place of burial: Swan Point Cemetery, Providence, Rhode Island

Benjamin Franklin Butler
Union

Date of birth: November 5, 1818

Birthplace: Deerfield, New Hampshire

U.S. Military Academy: no

Pre-war experience: Colby College, teacher, criminal lawyer, Massachusetts House and Senate

Rank: Major General

Major Battles and Campaigns: Big Bethel, Hatteras Inlet, occupied New Orleans, commander - Army of the James, Bermuda Hundred, Fort Fisher

Post-war achievements: U.S. House of Representatives, Governor of Massachusetts

Date of death: January 11, 1893

Place of burial: Lowell, Massachusetts

Joshua Lawrence Chamberlain
Union

Date of birth: September 8, 1828

Birthplace: Brewer, Maine

U.S. Military Academy: no

Pre-war experience: Bowdoin College, Bangor Theological Seminary, college professor

Rank: Lt. Colonel - 20th Maine, Colonel - same, Brig. General, Major General

Major Battles and Campaigns: Antietam, Fredericksburg, Chancellorsville, Little Round Top at Gettysburg, Spotsylvania, Cold Harbor (20th Maine); Petersburg, Five Forks, Appomattox (Brigade, V Corps); wounded six times during the war

Post-war achievements: Governor of Maine, college president, General in Maine militia, businessman, author

Date of death: February 24, 1914

Place of burial: Pine Grove Cemetery, Brunswick, Maine

Thomas James Churchill

Confederate

Date of birth: March 10, 1824

Birthplace: Jefferson County, Kentucky

U.S. Military Academy: no

Pre-war experience: St. Mary's College, Transylvania University, Mexican War, planter, postmaster of Little Rock, Ark.

Rank: Colonel - 1st Arkansas Mounted Rifles, Brig. General, Major General

Major Battles and Campaigns: Wilson's Creek (1st Arkansas); Richmond, Ky., Arkansas Post (Brigade); Red River Campaign - 1864, Jenkin's Ferry (Detachment)

Post-war achievements: Arkansas State Treasurer, Governor of Arkansas

Date of death: May 14, 1905

Place of burial: Mount Holly Cemetery, Little Rock, Arkansas

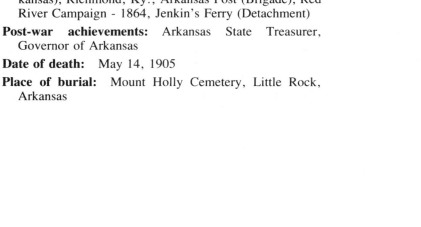

Karl Sundstrom

Patrick Ronayne Cleburne

Confederate

Date of birth: March 17, 1828

Birthplace: near Cork, Ireland

U.S. Military Academy: no

Pre-war experience: Her Majesty's Infantry, immigrated to the United States in 1849, pharmacist, lawyer

Rank: Captain, Colonel - 1st and 15th Arkansas, Brig. General, Major General

Major Battles and Campaigns: Shiloh, Perryville, Richmond, Ky. - wounded (Brigade); Stones River (Division, Hardee's Corps); Chickamauga (Division, D.H. Hill's Corps); Chattanooga (Division, Hardee's Corps); Atlanta Campaign (succeeded to command of Hardee's Corps); Franklin, Tn. - killed

Post-war achievements: none

Date of death: November 30, 1864

Place of burial: Helena, Arkansas

Samuel Wylie Crawford
Union

Date of birth: November 8, 1829

Birthplace: Franklin County, Pennsylvania

U.S. Military Academy: no

Pre-war experience: University of Pennsylvania – 1846, UP Medical School - 1850, assistant surgeon - U.S. Army, frontier duty, Fort Moultrie

Rank: Major - 13th U.S., Brig. General, Major General

Major Battles and Campaigns: Fort Sumter (Battery); Jackson's Shenandoah Valley Campaign, Cedar Mountain (Brigade); Antietam - wounded (Brigade/Division); Gettysburg, Wilderness, Spotsylvania, Jericho Mills, Bethesda Church, Petersburg, Globe Tavern, Five Forks (Division - V Corps)

Post-war achievements: served in the U.S. Army until 1873

Date of death: November 3, 1892

Place of burial: Laurel Hill Cemetery, Philadelphia, Pennsylvania

Thomas Leonidas Crittenden
Union

Date of birth: May 15, 1819

Birthplace: Russelville, Kentucky

U.S. Military Academy: no

Pre-war experience: lawyer, Mexican War - Colonel 3rd Kentucky, Consul to Liverpool, Louisville businessman

Rank: Brig. General, Major General

Major Battles and Campaigns: Shiloh (5th Division, Army of the Ohio); Stones River (Left Wing, Army of the Cumberland); Chickamauga (XXI Corps); resigned December 13, 1864

Post-war achievements: State Treasurer of Kentucky, Colonel - 32nd and 17th U.S. Infantry 1866-1881

Date of death: October 23, 1893

Place of burial: Frankfort, Kentucky

Samuel Ryan Curtis
Union

Date of birth: February 3, 1805

Birthplace: Clinton County, New York

U.S. Military Academy: Class of 1831 (27/33) Infantry

Pre-war experience: resigned from U.S. Army in 1832, civil engineer, Mexican War - Colonel of 2nd Ohio Vols., lawyer, Mayor of Keokuk, Iowa, U.S. House of Representatives

Rank: Colonel - 2nd Iowa, Brig. General, Major General

Major Battles and Campaigns: commanded camp of instruction near St. Louis; Pea Ridge (commanded Army of the Southwest); occupation of Helena, various Department commands

Post-war achievements: Indian and railroad commissioner

Date of death: December 26, 1866

Place of burial: Oakland Cemetery, Keokuk, Iowa

George Armstrong Custer
Union

Date of birth: December 5, 1839

Birthplace: New Rumley, Ohio

U.S. Military Academy: Class of June 1861 (34/34) Cavalry

Pre-war experience: student

Rank: 1st Lieutenant, Brig. General, Major General

Major Battles and Campaigns: from the First Manassas Campaign through to Appomattox, he took part in every battle of the Army of the Potomac except one; breveted for gallant services at Gettysburg, Yellow Tavern, Winchester, Fishers Hill and Five Forks (Brigade and Division Cavalry commands)

Post-war achievements: Indian fighter, killed at the Little Big Horn, Montana

Date of death: June 25, 1876

Place of burial: West Point, New York

Jefferson Columbus Davis
Union

Date of birth: March 2, 1828

Birthplace: Clark County, Indiana

U.S. Military Academy: no

Pre-war experience: Mexican War - private in 3rd Indiana, commissioned into regular Army in 1848, garrison duty

Rank: 1st Lt. & Capt. - 1st U.S. Art., Colonel - 22nd Indiana, Brig. Gen.

Major Battles and Campaigns: Ft. Sumter; Wilson's Creek (Brigade); Pea Ridge (3rd Division); Corinth (4th Division, Army of Mississippi); shot ex-commanding officer Gen. William Nelson; Stones River (Division, Army of the Cumberland); Chickamauga (Division); Atlanta Campaign, "March to the Sea," Carolinas Campaign (XIV Corps)

Post-war achievements: Colonel - 23rd U.S. Infantry, served in Alaska and the Modoc War

Date of death: November 30, 1879

Place of burial: Crown Hill Cemetery, Indianapolis, Indiana

Jefferson Finis Davis
Confederate

Date of birth: June 3, 1808

Birthplace: Christian (now Todd) County, Kentucky

U.S. Military Academy: Class of 1828 (23/33) Infantry-Dragoons

Pre-war experience: frontier duty, resigned from U.S. Army in 1835 to become a planter in Mississippi, U.S. House of Representatives, Mexican War, U.S. Senator, Secretary of War under Pierce 1853-1857, again U.S. Senator until 1861

Rank: Major General of Mississippi State Militia

Major Battles and Campaigns: Provisional President (February 1861) and President by popular vote (November 1861) of the Confederate States of America. Inaugurated February 22, 1862 at Richmond, Va., to serve for six years. Captured at Irwinsville, Georgia on May 10, 1865

Post-war achievements: confined for two years at Fort Monroe, Virginia; unsuccessful businessman, writer

Date of death: December 9, 1889

Place of burial: originally in New Orleans, Louisiana until reinterred in Hollywood Cemetery, Richmond, Virginia in 1893

Abner Doubleday

Union

Date of birth: June 26, 1819

Birthplace: Ballston Spa, New York

U.S. Military Academy: Class of 1842 (24/56) Artillery-Infantry

Pre-war experience: civil engineer, Seminole and Mexican Wars, allegedly the inventor of modern baseball

Rank: Captain, Brig. General, Major General

Major Battles and Campaigns: Fort Sumter; Second Manassas (Brigade, III Corps, Army of Virginia); Antietam, Fredericksburg (Division, III Corps); in reserve at Chancellorsville, Gettysburg (Division I Corps, temporarily in command of I Corps after death of Reynolds); administrative duties in Washington, D.C.

Post-war achievements: Colonel - 35th U.S. Infantry, author

Date of death: January 26, 1893

Place of burial: Arlington National Cemetery

Jubal Anderson Early

Confederate

Date of birth: November 3, 1816

Birthplace: Franklin County, Virginia

U.S. Military Academy: Class of 1837 (18/50) Artillery

Pre-war experience: Seminole War, resigned from U.S. Army in 1838, lawyer, Delegator in Virginia House, Commonwealth attorney, Mexican War service with Virginia Volunteers

Rank: Colonel - 24th Virginia, Brig. General, Major General, Lt. General

Major Battles and Campaigns: First Manassas (6th Brigade); Williamsburg - wounded, Second Manassas (Brigade); Antietam, Fredericksburg (Ewell's Division); Chancellorsville, Gettysburg, Wilderness, Spotsylvania (Division); Cold Harbor (II Corps); Raid on Washington, Monocacy, Winchester, Fisher's Hill, Cedar Creek (independent operations with II Corps)

Post-war achievements: lawyer, first President of the Southern Historical Society, supervisor of Louisiana Lottery, writer, opponent of James Longstreet

Date of death: March 2, 1894

Place of burial: Lynchburg, Virginia

Richard Stoddert Ewell

Confederate

Date of birth: February 8, 1817

Birthplace: Georgetown, District of Columbia

U.S. Military Academy: Class of 1840 (13/42) Dragoons

Pre-war experience: Mexican War, frontier duty and Indian fighting, resigned from U.S. Army on June 17, 1861

Rank: Brig. General, Major General, Lt. General

Major Battles and Campaigns: First Manassas (2nd Brigade); Jackson's Shenandoah Valley Campaign, Seven Days, Second Manassas - wounded (Division); Gettysburg, Kelly's Ford - wounded, Wilderness, Spotsylvania (Corps); Richmond defenses (commanded Department of Henrico); Sayler's Creek - captured

Post-war achievements: none

Date of death: January 25, 1872

Place of burial: Old City Cemetery, Nashville, Tennessee

David Glasgow Farragut

Union

Date of birth: July 5, 1801

Birthplace: near Knoxville, Tennessee

U.S. Military Academy: no

Pre-war experience: entered the Navy as a Midshipman in 1810/11 and began his long naval career, brief service in Mexican War, ordnance duty in the 1850's, established the Mare Island, California, Navy Yard

Rank: Captain, Rear Admiral, Vice Admiral

Major Battles and Campaigns: New Orleans - Forts Jackson and St. Philip, Mississippi River - Vicksburg and Port Hudson, Mobile Bay

Post-war achievements: first officer in the U.S. Navy to be promoted to the rank of Full Admiral (July 25, 1866), traveler

Date of death: August 14, 1870

Place of burial: Woodlawn Cemetery, Westchester County, New York

John Buchanan Floyd

Confederate

Date of birth: June 1, 1806

Birthplace: Montgomery County, Virginia

U.S. Military Academy: no

Pre-war experience: South Carolina College, lawyer, cotton planter, Delegator in Virginia House, Governor of Virginia 1848-1852, Secretary of War under Buchanan 1857-1860

Rank: Brig. General, Major General of Virginia State Troops

Major Battles and Campaigns: West Virginia (Brigade); Fort Donelson (commander, his flight from the Fort before it was surrendered led to his removal from command of troops)

Post-war achievements: none, died of natural causes

Date of death: August 26, 1863

Place of burial: Abingdon, Virginia

Bill Turner

Eleanor S. Brockenbrough Library   Museum of the Confederacy

John Horace Forney

Confederate

Date of birth: August 12, 1829

Birthplace: Lincolnton, North Carolina

U.S. Military Academy: Class of 1852 (22/43) Infantry

Pre-war experience: garrison and frontier duty, Utah Expedition; instructor at West Point, resigned from U.S. Army on January 23, 1861

Rank: Colonel - 10th Ala., Brig. General, Major General

Major Battles and Campaigns: First Manassas, Dranesville - severely wounded (Regiment); departmental commands in Alabama and Florida; Vicksburg - captured (Division); served in Trans-Mississippi Department

Post-war achievements: planter and civil engineer in Alabama

Date of death: September 13, 1902

Place of burial: Jacksonville, Alabama

18

Nathan Bedford Forrest
Confederate

Date of birth: July 13, 1821

Birthplace: Bedford County, Tennessee

U.S. Military Academy: no

Pre-war experience: very little formal schooling, rose from poverty to become a successful businessman in real estate, cotton, livestock and slaves

Rank: Private - 7th Tennessee Cavalry, Lt. Colonel of a battalion of mounted troops he raised and equipped, Colonel - 3rd Tennessee, Brig. General, Major General, Lt. General

Major Battles and Campaigns: Fort Donelson, Shiloh, Chickamauga, Chattanooga, Fort Pillow, Brice's Cross Roads, Tupelo, Franklin, Nashville, Selma; numerous independent raids in Tennessee disrupting the flow of Federal supplies and communications in 1862-1864

Post-war achievements: planter, railroad president

Date of death: October 29, 1877

Place of burial: Memphis, Tennessee

William Buel Franklin
Union

Date of birth: February 27, 1823

Birthplace: York, Pennsylvania

U.S. Military Academy: Class of 1843 (1/39) Engineers

Pre-war experience: Great Lakes survey 1843-45, Kearny's exploration of South Pass in the Rockies, Mexican War, instructor at West Point, construction projects in Washington, D.C.

Rank: Colonel - 12th U.S. Inf., Brig. General, Major General

Major Battles and Campaigns: First Manassas (1st Brigade, 3rd Division); Yorktown (Division); Peninsula Campaign, South Mountain, Antietam (VI Corps); Fredericksburg (Left Grand Division - I & VI Corps); Red River Campaign - wounded at Sabine Cross Roads (XIX Corps)

Post-war achievements: vice president and general manager of Colt's Patent Fire Arms Mfg. Co. for 22 years, presidential elector 1876, commissioner general for U.S. at Paris Exposition 1888

Date of death: March 8, 1903

Place of burial: York, Pennsylvania

John Charles Fremont

Union

Date of birth: January 21, 1813

Birthplace: Savannah, Georgia

U.S. Military Academy: no

Pre-war experience: attended Charleston College, S.C., mathematics teacher, 2nd Lt. - U.S. Army Corps of Topographical Engineers 1838, explorer in western U.S., conquest of California 1846, elected Governor of California by settlers, resigned from U.S. Army in 1848 after a court-martial on charges of mutiny and insubordination, U.S. Senator from California, Republican Presidential nominee in 1856

Rank: Major General

Major Battles and Campaigns: commanded the Department of the West - 1861; Jackson's Shenandoah Valley Campaign - 1862; June 1862 to June 1864 he was "waiting orders" in New York, resigned from U.S. Army on June 4, 1864

Post-war achievements: nominated for President in 1864, but withdrew; railroad financier, Territorial Governor of Arizona 1878-1887

Date of death: July 13, 1890

Place of burial: Rockland Cemetery, Piedmont-on-the-Hudson, New York

James Abram Garfield

Union

Date of birth: November 19, 1831

Birthplace: Orange, Ohio

U.S. Military Academy: no

Pre-war experience: Williams College, professor, Ohio State Senator

Rank: Lt. Colonel & Colonel - 42nd Ohio, Brig. General, Major General

Major Battles and Campaigns: Middle Creek and Pound Gap, KY (Brigade); Shiloh - 2nd day (Brigade); served on Fitz-John Porter's court-martial; Chickamauga (Rosecrans' Chief of Staff)

Post-war achievements: U.S. House of Representatives 1863-1880, elected U.S. Senator 1880, elected 20th President of the United States 1880; shot by Charles J. Guiteau in Washington 1881 and died eleven weeks later

Date of death: September 19, 1881

Place of burial: Lakeview Cemetery, Cleveland, Ohio

Wendell W. Lang, Jr.

John White Geary
Union

Date of birth: December 30, 1819

Birthplace: Mount Pleasant, Pennsylvania

U.S. Military Academy: no

Pre-war experience: attended Jefferson College, teacher, clerk, lawyer, surveyor, Mexican War - 2nd Pennsylvania, organized postal service in California, Mayor of San Francisco, Governor of Kansas 1856

Rank: Colonel - 28th Pennsylvania, Brig. General

Major Battles and Campaigns: wounded at Harpers Ferry October 1861; captured at Leesburg March 1862; Cedar Mountain - wounded twice (Brigade, II Corps); Chancellorsville, Gettysburg, Wauhatchie, Chattanooga (Division, XII Corps); "March to the Sea", Carolinas Campaign (Division, XX Corps)

Post-war achievements: Military Governor of Savannah, Governor of Pennsylvania 1867-1873

Date of death: January 18, 1873

Place of burial: Harrisburg, Pennsylvania

John Gibbon
Union

Date of birth: April 20, 1827

Birthplace: Philadelphia, Pennsylvania

U.S. Military Academy: Class of 1847 (20/38) Artillery

Pre-war experience: Mexican and Seminole Wars, artillery instructor at West Point, wrote "The Artillerist's Manual"

Rank: Captain, Brig. General, Major General

Major Battles and Campaigns: Second Manassas (Brigade, III Corps, Army of Virginia); Antietam (Brigade, I Corps); Fredericksburg - wounded (Division, I Corps); Marye's Heights, Gettysburg - wounded (Division, II Corps)); commanded draft depots in Cleveland, Ohio and Philadelphia, Pa.; Wilderness, Spotsylvania, North Anna, Cold Harbor, Petersburg (Division, II Corps; XVIII and XXIV Corps); Appomattox

Post-war achievements: Colonel - 36th and 7th U.S. Infantry regiments, Indian fighting, led the relief column to the Little Big Horn in 1876 and buried the dead, against the Nez Perces in 1877, retired in 1891, Commander-in-Chief of the Loyal Legion, writer

Date of death: February 6, 1896

Place of burial: Arlington National Cemetery

Quincy Adams Gillmore

Union

Date of birth: February 28, 1825

Birthplace: Lorain, Ohio

U.S. Military Academy: Class of 1849 (1/43) Engineers

Pre-war experience: supervised harbor fortification construction at Hampton Roads and New York City, instructor at West Point

Rank: Captain, Brig. General, Major General

Major Battles and Campaigns: Port Royal Expedition (Chief Engineer); Fort Pulaski (directed placement of batteries to reduce the Fort); Forts Wagner and Gregg, Charleston (commanded X Corps and Department of the South); Bermuda Hundred, Drewry's Bluff (X Corps); Early's Shenandoah Valley Campaign (2 divisions, XIX Corps) - injured in fall from horse; commanded Department of the South from February - June 1865

Post-war achievements: served in the U.S. Army on numerous boards and commissions, author, president of Mississippi River Commission

Date of death: April 7, 1888

Place of burial: West Point, New York

John Brown Gordon

Confederate

Date of birth: February 6, 1832

Birthplace: Upson County, Georgia

U.S. Military Academy: no

Pre-war experience: attended University of Georgia, lawyer, coal mine developer

Rank: Captain - "Raccoon Roughs", Colonel - 6th Alabama, Brig. General, Major General

Major Battles and Campaigns: Peninsular Campaign (6th Alabama then a Brigade); Antietam - wounded (6th Alabama); Chancellorsville, Gettysburg, Wilderness, Spotsylvania (Brigade); Early's Shenandoah Valley Campaign, Petersburg, Fort Stedman, Appomattox (Division)

Post-war achievements: U.S. Senator from Georgia - three times, Governor of Georgia 1886-1890, writer, first commander-in-chief of the United Confederate Veterans 1890-1904

Date of death: January 9, 1904

Place of burial: Oakland Cemetery, Atlanta, Georgia

Gordon Granger
Union

Date of birth: November 6, 1822

Birthplace: Joy, Wayne County, New York

U.S. Military Academy: Class of 1845 (35/41) Infantry - Mounted Rifles

Pre-war experience: Mexican War, western frontier duty

Rank: Captain - 3rd U.S. Cav., Colonel - 2nd Mich. Cav., Brig. General, Major General

Major Battles and Campaigns: Wilson's Creek, New Madrid, Island No. 10, Corinth; Chickamauga (Reserve Corps); Missionary Ridge, Knoxville (IV Corps); Forts Gaines and Morgan, capture of Mobile (XIII Corps)

Post-war achievements: Colonel - 25th U.S. Infantry, commanded District of Memphis and District of New Mexico

Date of death: January 10, 1876

Place of burial: Lexington, Kentucky

Ulysses Simpson Grant
Union

Date of birth: April 27, 1822

Birthplace: Point Pleasant, Ohio

U.S. Military Academy: Class of 1843 (21/39) Infantry

Pre-war experience: Mexican War, duty in Pacific Northwest, resigned from U.S. Army on July 31, 1854, farmer, salesman, clerk

Rank: Colonel - 21st Illinois, Brig. General, Major General, Lt. General

Major Battles and Campaigns: Belmont, Mo., Forts Henry and Donelson, Shiloh, Vicksburg, Chattanooga, with Meade's Army of the Potomac from the Wilderness to Appomattox, named General-in-Chief of the Armies of the United States on March 12, 1864

Post-war achievements: President of the United States 1868-1875, unsuccessful businessman, autobiographer

Date of death: July 23, 1885

Place of burial: New York City, New York

Henry Wager Halleck

Union

Date of birth: January 16, 1815

Birthplace: Westernville, New York

U.S. Military Academy: Class of 1839 (3/31) Engineers

Pre-war experience: Hudson Academy, Union College, assistant professor at West Point while still an undergraduate, author and lecturer on military science and defense, Mexican War service in California - military government assignments, lawyer, businessman and publisher of legal books

Rank: Major General

Major Battles and Campaigns: commanded the Department of the Missouri and the Department of the Mississippi, "captured" Corinth, General-in-Chief 1862-1864, Chief of Staff after U.S. Grant's promotion to Lt. General

Post-war achievements: served in the U.S. Army in command of various military divisions

Date of death: January 9, 1872

Place of burial: Green-Wood Cemetery, Brooklyn, New York

Wade Hampton

Confederate

Date of birth: March 28, 1818

Birthplace: Charleston, South Carolina

U.S. Military Academy: no

Pre-war experience: South Carolina College, very successful landowner and planter, served in South Carolina legislature

Rank: Colonel - Hampton Legion, Brig. General, Major General, Lt. General

Major Battles and Campaigns: First Manassas - wounded; Peninsular Campaign - wounded at Seven Pines; Antietam, Stuart's operations, Gettysburg - wounded (Brigade level); Petersburg (commanded cavalry, Army of Northern Virginia); from January 1865 with J. E. Johnston in the Carolinas

Post-war achievements: businessman, Governor of South Carolina, U.S. Senator from South Carolina 1879-1891, railroad commissioner

Date of death: April 11, 1902

Place of burial: Columbia, South Carolina

Winfield Scott Hancock

Union

Date of birth: February 14, 1824

Birthplace: Montgomery Square near Norristown, Pennsylvania

U.S. Military Academy: Class of 1840 (18/25) Infantry

Pre-war experience: Mexican and Seminole Wars, Utah Expedition, Chief Quartermaster in Los Angeles, California

Rank: Captain, Brig. General, Major General

Major Battles and Campaigns: Peninsular Campaign, Antietam (Brigades IV and VI Corps); Fredericksburg, Chancellorsville (Division, II Corps); Gettysburg - wounded, Wilderness, Spotsylvania, Cold Harbor, Petersburg (II Corps); from November 1864 he commanded various military departments due to disability for field command because of wound

Post-war achievements: served in the U.S. Army and eventually commanded the Department of the East, Democratic nominee for President in 1880

Date of death: February 9, 1886

Place of burial: Montgomery Cemetery, Norristown, Pennsylvania

William Joseph Hardee

Confederate

Date of birth: October 12, 1815

Birthplace: Camden County, Georgia

U.S. Military Academy: Class of 1838 (26/45) Dragoons

Pre-war experience: Seminole and Mexican Wars, Commandant of Cadets at West Point, author of tactics manual, resigned from U.S. Army on January 31, 1861

Rank: Colonel C.S.A., Brig. General, Major General, Lt. General

Major Battles and Campaigns: Shiloh, Perryville, Stones River, Chattanooga, Atlanta Campaign (Corps); "March to the Sea", Carolinas Campaign (commanded Department of South Carolina, Georgia, and Florida)

Post-war achievements: planter

Date of death: November 6, 1873

Place of burial: Selma, Alabama

Benjamin Harrison

Union

Date of birth: August 20, 1833

Birthplace: North Bend, Ohio

U.S. Military Academy: no

Pre-war experience: Miami Univ. of Ohio; lawyer; Indianapolis, IN City Attorney; Reporter, Indiana Supreme Court

Rank: 2nd Lt., Captain, Colonel - 70th Indiana, Bvt. Brig. General

Major Battles and Campaigns: Atlanta Campaign - Resaca, New Hope Church, Kennesaw Mountain, Peach Tree Creek; "March to the Sea"; Carolinas Campaign - Bentonville; surrender of Johnston

Post-war achievements: corporation lawyer, United States Senator 1881-1887, elected 23rd President of the United States 1888

Date of death: March 13, 1901

Place of burial: Indianapolis, Indiana

Rutherford Birchard Hayes

Union

Date of birth: October 4, 1822

Birthplace: Delaware, Ohio

U.S. Military Academy: no

Pre-war experience: Kenyon College, Harvard Law School, attorney

Rank: Major - 23rd Ohio, Lt. Colonel, Colonel, Brig. General, Bvt. Major General

Major Battles and Campaigns: Antietam Campaign - wounded at South Mountain; capture of Confederate General Morgan; Shenandoah Valley Campaign - Winchester, Cedar Creek (Brigade, Division)

Post-war achievements: U.S. House of Representatives 1865-1867, Govenor of Ohio 1868-1872 and 1876-1877, elected 19th President of the United States 1877, lecturer

Date of death: January 17, 1893

Place of burial: Spiegel Grove, Fremont, Ohio

Henry Heth

Confederate

Date of birth: December 16, 1825

Birthplace: Chesterfield County, Virginia

U.S. Military Academy: Class of 1847 (38/38) Infantry

Pre-war experience: Mexican War, frontier service, resigned from U.S. Army on April 25, 1861

Rank: Captain, Major, Lt. Colonel; Colonel - 45th Virginia, Brig. General

Major Battles and Campaigns: West Virginia; Kentucky campaign; Chancellorsville (Brigade, Hill's Corps); Gettysburg - wounded, Wilderness, Spotsylvania, Cold Harbor, Petersburg (Division, Hill's Corps); Appomattox

Post-war achievements: insurance businessman, holder of minor government positions

Date of death: September 27, 1899

Place of burial: Hollywood Cemetery, Richmond, Virginia

Ambrose Powell Hill

Confederate

Date of birth: November 9, 1825

Birthplace: Culpeper, Virginia

U.S. Military Academy: Class of 1847 (15/38) Artillery

Pre-war experience: Mexican and Seminole Wars, frontier duty, resigned from U.S. Army on March 1, 1861

Rank: Colonel - 13th Virginia, Brig. General, Major General

Major Battles and Campaigns: reserve at First Manassas (13th Virginia); Peninsular Campaign (Division, Longstreet's Corps); Cedar Mountain, Second Manassas, Harpers Ferry, Antietam, Fredericksburg, Chancellorsville - wounded (Division, Jackson's Corps); Gettysburg, Wilderness, North Anna, Cold Harbor, Petersburg - killed in action (III Corps)

Post-war achievements: none

Date of death: April 2, 1865

Place of burial: Richmond, Virginia

Daniel Harvey Hill

Confederate

Date of birth: July 12, 1821

Birthplace: York District, South Carolina

U.S. Military Academy: Class of 1842 (28/56) Artillery - Infantry

Pre-war experience: border and garrison duty, Mexican War, resigned from U.S. Army in 1849, college professor, superintendent of the North Carolina Military Institute

Rank: Colonel - 1st N.C., Brig. General, Major General, Lt. General

Major Battles and Campaigns: Big Bethel; Yorktown, Williamsburg, Seven Pines, Seven Days, Second Manassas, South Mountain, Antietam (Division); command of Dept. of N.C.; defended Richmond during Gettysburg campaign; Chickamauga (Corps); Bentonville (Division); surrender of Johnston

Post-war achievements: magazine editor, president of the University of Arkansas 1877-1884 and the Georgia Military Academy 1885-1889

Date of death: September 24, 1889

Place of burial: Davidson College Cemetery, Davidson, North Carolina

Civil War Library and Museum

John Bell Hood

Confederate

Date of birth: June 1, 1831

Birthplace: Owingsville, Kentucky

U.S. Military Academy: Class of 1853 (44/52) Infantry

Pre-war experience: garrison and frontier duty, wounded in Indian fighting, resigned from U.S. Army on April 17, 1861

Rank: 1st Lieutenant to Brig. General, Major General, Lt. General, Full General (temporary rank)

Major Battles and Campaigns: Peninsular Campaign, Second Manassas, Antietam (Texas Brigade); Fredericksburg, Gettysburg - wounded (Division, Longstreet's Corps); Chickamauga - wounded (commanded Longstreet's Corps plus three divisions); Atlanta Campaign, Franklin, Nashville (commanded Corps until July 1864 when he succeeded J.E. Johnston to command of the Army of Tennessee); surrendered at Natchez, Mississippi in May 1865

Post-war achievements: merchant

Date of death: August 30, 1879

Place of burial: Metairie Cemetery, New Orleans, Louisiana

28

Joseph Hooker
Union

Date of birth: November 13, 1814

Birthplace: Hadley, Massachusetts

U.S. Military Academy: Class of 1837 (29/50) Artillery

Pre-war experience: Seminole and Mexican Wars, staff assignments, resigned from U.S. Army on February 21, 1853, farmer

Rank: Brig. General, Major General

Major Battles and Campaigns: Peninsular Campaign, Bristoe Station, Second Manassas, Chantilly (Division, III Corps); Antietam - wounded (I Corps); Fredericksburg (Centre Grand Division); Chancellorsville (commanded the Army of the Potomac); Chattanooga, Atlanta Campaign (XX Corps)

Post-war achievements: Departmental army commands

Date of death: October 31, 1879

Place of burial: Cincinnati, Ohio

Oliver Otis Howard
Union

Date of birth: November 30, 1830

Birthplace: Leeds, Maine

U.S. Military Academy: Class of 1854 (4/46) Ordnance

Pre-war experience: Bowdoin College, assistant professor at West Point, ordnance duty

Rank: Colonel - 3rd Maine, Brig. General, Major General

Major Battles and Campaigns: First Manassas (Brigade, Heintzelman's Division); Peninsular Campaign - wounded twice at Seven Pines, Second Manassas, Antietam (Brigade, II Corps); Fredericksburg (Division, II Corps); Chancellorsville, Gettysburg, Chattanooga (XI Corps); Atlanta Campaign - wounded at Pickett's Mill (IV Corps); Fall of Atlanta, "March to the Sea", Carolinas Campaign, Bentonville (commanded the Army of the Tennessee from July 1864)

Post-war achievements: first commissioner of the "Freedmen's Bureau", bank director, served in Indian country, helped found Howard University, superintendent of West Point, various departmental commands, aided to establish Lincoln Memorial University, author, speaker

Date of death: October 26, 1909

Place of burial: Lake View Cemetery, Burlington, Vermont

Henry Jackson Hunt

Union

Date of birth: September 14, 1819

Birthplace: Detroit, Michigan

U.S. Military Academy: Class of 1839 (19/31) Artillery

Pre-war experience: Mexican War, served on board to revise light artillery tactics

Rank: Major - 5th U.S. Artillery, Colonel, Brig. General, Major General

Major Battles and Campaigns: First Manassas (Battery); Peninsular Campaign, Malvern Hill (commanded Reserve Artillery); Antietam, Fredericksburg, Chancellorsville, Gettysburg, Wilderness, Spotsylvania, Cold Harbor (Chief of Artillery, Army of the Potomac); Petersburg (in charge of all siege operations)

Post-war achievements: various military District and Department commands, Governor of the Soldier's Home

Date of death: February 11, 1889

Place of burial: Soldier's Home, Washington, D.C.

David Hunter

Union

Date of birth: July 21, 1802

Birthplace: Washington, D.C.

U.S. Military Academy: Class of 1822 (25/40) Infantry-Dragoons

Pre-war experience: frontier duty, resigned from U.S. Army in 1836 to speculate in real estate, returned to the Army in 1842 and in 1860 was stationed in Kansas, accompanied President-elect Lincoln to Washington, D.C.

Rank: Colonel - 3rd U.S. Cavalry, Brig. General, Major General

Major Battles and Campaigns: First Manassas - wounded (2nd Division); Fort Pulaski, Secessionville (commanded Department of the South); various boards and commissions; Early's Shenandoah Valley Campaign, Lynchburg

Post-war achievements: accompanied Abraham Lincoln's body to Springfield, Illinois, presided at the trial of the Lincoln conspirators

Date of death: February 2, 1886

Place of burial: Princeton, New Jersey

Thomas Jonathan Jackson
Confederate

Date of birth: January 21, 1824

Birthplace: Clarksburg, Virginia (now West Virginia)

U.S. Military Academy: Class of 1846 (17/59) Artillery

Pre-war experience: Mexican War, resigned from U.S. Army in 1851/52 to become an instructor at the Virginia Military Institute

Rank: Colonel, Brig. General, Major General, Lt. General

Major Battles and Campaigns: First Manassas - earned nickname "Stonewall" (Brigade); Shenandoah Valley Campaign, Seven Days, Second Manassas, Harpers Ferry, Antietam (Division); Fredericksburg, Chancellorsville (Corps) - wounded May 2, 1863 by his own men and died of pneumonia after amputation of his left arm

Post-war achievements: none

Date of death: May 10, 1863

Place of burial: Lexington, Virginia

Andrew Johnson
Union

Date of birth: December 29, 1808

Birthplace: Raleigh, North Carolina

U.S. Military Academy: no

Pre-war experience: moved to Tennessee at age 18, tailor, alderman, mayor, Tennessee State Legislator, U.S. Congressman, Governor of Tennessee, U.S. Senator

Rank: Brig. General

Major Battles and Campaigns: the only U.S. Senator from the eleven seceded states who kept his seat and adhered to the Union; Military Governor of Tennessee from March 4, 1862, organized loyal government in the state; nominated Vice-President with Lincoln in 1864; President of the United States (April 1865) after Lincoln's assassination

Post-war achievements: resolved to carry out Lincoln's conciliatory Reconstruction plans, survived impeachment proceedings by Radical Republicans in 1868, U.S. Senator from Tennessee

Date of death: July 31, 1875

Place of burial: Andrew Johnson National Cemetery, Greeneville, Tennessee

Bushrod Rust Johnson

Confederate

Date of birth: October 7, 1817

Birthplace: Belmont County, Ohio

U.S. Military Academy: Class of 1840 (23/42) Infantry

Pre-war experience: Seminole War, Mexican War, frontier duty, resigned from U.S. Army in 1847; teacher, superintendent of Military College of Univ. of Nashville, active in state militia

Rank: Colonel, Brig. General, Major General

Major Battles and Campaigns: Fort Donelson; Shiloh - wounded, Perryville, Stones River (Brigade); Chickamauga, Knoxville (Division); Wilderness, Petersburg, Drewry's Bluff, Saylor's Creek (Division); Appomattox

Post-war achievements: chancellor of the Univ. of Nashville

Date of death: September 12, 1880

Place of burial: Miles Station, Illinois

author's collection

Edward Johnson

Confederate

Date of birth: April 16, 1816

Birthplace: Salisbury, Chesterfield County, Virginia

U.S. Military Academy: Class of 1838 (32/45) Infantry

Pre-war experience: Seminole and Mexican Wars, frontier service, resigned from U.S. Army on June 10, 1861

Rank: Colonel - 12th Virginia, Brig. General, Major General

Major Battles and Campaigns: Jackson's Shenandoah Valley Campaign - severely wounded (Brigade); Gettysburg, Wilderness, Spotsylvania - captured at the "Bloody Angle" (Division); Franklin, Nashville - captured (Division, S.D. Lee's Corps)

Post-war achievements: farmer

Date of death: March 2, 1873

Place of burial: Hollywood Cemetery, Richmond, Virginia

Joseph Eggleston Johnston
Confederate

Date of birth: February 3, 1807

Birthplace: Farmville, Virginia

U.S. Military Academy: Class of 1829 (13/46) Artillery

Pre-war experience: Black Hawk and Seminole Wars, resigned from U.S. Army in 1837, civil engineer, re-enlisted as 1st Lt. in 1838, Mexican War - wounded five times, frontier duty in Texas and Kansas with engineers and cavalry, Utah Expedition, resigned from U.S. Army on April 22, 1861

Rank: Brig. General, Full General

Major Battles and Campaigns: First Manassas (Commander); Peninsular Campaign, Seven Pines - severely wounded (commanded Army of Northern Virginia, replaced by R.E. Lee); November 1862 named commander Department of the West - subordinates fought at Stones River, Vicksburg, Chickamauga and Chattanooga; Atlanta Campaign (commanded Army of Tennessee from December 1863-July 1864 until replaced by J.B. Hood); Carolinas Campaign (commanded the Army of Tennessee), surrendered to Sherman on April 26, 1865

Post-war achievements: insurance businessman, U.S. Congressman from Virginia, railroad commissioner, writer

Date of death: March 21, 1891

Place of burial: Green Mount Cemetery, Baltimore, Maryland

Albert Sidney Johnston
Confederate

Date of birth: February 2, 1803

Birthplace: Washington, Kentucky

U.S. Military Academy: Class of 1826 (8/41) Infantry

Pre-war experience: Black Hawk War, resigned from U.S. Army in 1834, enlisted as a private in the Texas Army in 1836, rose to senior Brig. General, Secretary of War of the Republic of Texas, Colonel of Texas volunteers in Mexican War, became Colonel in U.S. Cavalry, led Utah Expedition, command Departments of Texas, Utah, and the Pacific, resigned from the U.S. Army on May 3, 1861

Rank: Full General

Major Battles and Campaigns: commanded all Confederate troops west of the Allegheny Mountains from August 1861; subordinates defeated at Logan Cross Roads and lost Forts Henry and Donelson; attacked U.S. Grant at Shiloh - mortally wounded in leg

Post-war achievements: none

Date of death: April 6, 1862

Place of burial: originally in Meterie Cemetery, New Orleans, Louisiana until reinterred in the State Cemetery, Austin, Texas after the war

Joseph Brevard Kershaw

Confederate

Date of birth: January 5, 1822

Birthplace: Camden, South Carolina

U.S. Military Academy: no

Pre-war experience: lawyer, Mexican War - Lt. of the Palmetto Regt., S.C. state legislator

Rank: Colonel - 2nd S.C., Brig. General, Major General

Major Battles and Campaigns: Fort Sumter, First Manassas; Peninsula Campaign, Second Manassas, South Mountain, Antietam, Fredericksburg, Chancellorsville, Gettysburg (Brigade); Chickamauga, Wilderness, Spotsylvania, Cold Harbor, Petersburg, Saylor's Creek - captured (Division)

Post-war achievements: lawyer, S.C. state senator, judge 1877-1893, postmaster of Camden, S.C.

Date of death: April 13, 1894

Place of burial: Camden, South Carolina

Hugh Judson Kilpatrick

Union

Date of birth: January 14, 1836

Birthplace: near Deckertown, New Jersey

U.S. Military Academy: Class of May 1861 (17/45) Artillery-Cavalry

Pre-war experience: student

Rank: 1st Lieutenant, Captain - 5th New York Inf., Lt. Colonel - 2nd New York Cavalry, Colonel - same, Brig. General

Major Battles and Campaigns: Big Bethel - wounded (5th N.Y.); Second Manassas (2nd N.Y.); Stoneman's Raid, Aldie, Middleburg, Upperville (Brigade, Cavalry Corps, Army of the Potomac); Hanover, Hunterstown, Gettysburg (3rd Division, Cavalry Corps); Kilpatrick/Dahlgren Raid; Atlanta Campaign - wounded (3rd Division, Cavalry Corps, Army of the Cumberland); "March to the Sea", Carolinas Campaign (3rd Division, Cavalry Corps, Military Division of Mississippi)

Post-war achievements: Minister to Chile (twice); politically active as a Democrat and as a Republican

Date of death: December 4, 1881

Place of burial: West Point, New York

Fitzhugh Lee
Confederate

Date of birth: November 19, 1835

Birthplace: Fairfax County, Virginia

U.S. Military Academy: Class of 1856 (45/49) Cavalry

Pre-war experience: frontier duty, Indian fighting - wounded, assistant instructor at West Point, resigned from U.S. Army on May 21, 1861, nephew of Robert E. Lee

Rank: 1st Lieutenant, Lt. Colonel - 1st Virginia Cavalry, Colonel - same, Brig. General, Major General

Major Battles and Campaigns: First Manassas (J.E. Johnston's staff); Peninsular Campaign, Antietam, Gettysburg (with JEB Stuart's Cavalry); Spotsylvania, Early's Shenandoah Valley Campaign - wounded at Winchester; returned to duty January 1865, Chief of Cavalry of the Army of Northern Virginia at Appomattox, surrendered April 11, 1865

Post-war achievements: farmer, Governor of Virginia 1885-1889, Consul General at Havana, Cuba, Major General of U.S. Volunteers during the Spanish-American War, Army Departmental commander, writer

Date of death: April 28, 1905

Place of burial: Hollywood Cemetery, Richmond, Virginia

Robert Edward Lee
Confederate

Date of birth: January 19, 1807

Birthplace: Westmoreland County, Virginia

U.S. Military Academy: Class of 1829 (2/46) Engineers

Pre-war experience: engineering assignments with U.S. Army on Atlantic coast and the Mississippi, Mexican War - wounded, Superintendent of West Point 1852-1855, frontier duty in Texas with 2nd U.S. Cavalry, on leave in Washington he was ordered to Harpers Ferry and was present at capture of John Brown in October 1859, resigned from U.S. Army on April 20, 1861

Rank: Commander-in-Chief of the Military and Naval Forces of Virginia, Brig. General, Full General

Major Battles and Campaigns: Cheat Mountain, South Atlantic coast, military advisor to President Davis, Seven Days (succeeded to command of the Army of Northern Virginia after the wounding of J.E. Johnston, a position he held until the surrender at Appomattox); Second Manassas, Antietam, Fredericksburg, Chancellorsville, Gettysburg, Wilderness, Spotsylvania, Cold Harbor, Petersburg, Appomattox - surrendered April 9, 1865 (Commander-in-Chief of all Confederate Armies since January 23, 1865)

Post-war achievements: President of Washington College, Lexington, Virginia (now Washington and Lee University)

Date of death: October 12, 1870

Place of burial: Lexington, Virginia

Stephen Dill Lee
Confederate

Date of birth: September 22, 1833

Birthplace: Charleston, South Carolina

U.S. Military Academy: Class of 1854 (17/46) Artillery

Pre-war experience: frontier duty, resigned from U.S. Army on February 20, 1861, no relation to the Virginia Lees

Rank: Captain, Major, Lt. Colonel, Colonel, Brig. General, Major General, Lt. General

Major Battles and Campaigns: Fort Sumter, Seven Days, Second Manassas, Antietam; Vicksburg - captured (Chief of Pemberton's Artillery); commander of cavalry in the Department of Mississippi, Alabama, West Tennessee and East Louisiana; Atlanta Campaign (succeeded to command of Hood's Corps); Franklin, Nashville - wounded, surrendered with J.E. Johnston

Post-war achievements: farmer, State Senator in Mississippi, first president of Mississippi State College, commissioner to organize Vicksburg National Military Park, commander-in-chief of the United Confederate Veterans 1904-1908

Date of death: May 28, 1908

Place of burial: Columbus, Mississippi

Abraham Lincoln
Union

Date of birth: February 12, 1809

Birthplace: near Hodgenville, Kentucky

U.S. Military Academy: no

Pre-war experience: little formal education, 1816 - family moves to Indiana, 1830 - family moves to Illinois, 1832 - elected Captain of volunteer company during Black Hawk War (no action), 1834 - elected to Illinois State Legislature, 1836 - lawyer, 1847 - U.S. Congressman from Illinois, 1858 - debated Stephen A. Douglas for U.S. Senate seat (unsuccessful), 1860 - nominated and won U.S. Presidential election as Republican

Rank: President - 16th, Commander-in-Chief

Major Battles and Campaigns: Inaugurated March 4, 1861; called for troops to defend the Union in April 1861; September 22, 1862 - issued preliminary Emancipation Proclamation; November 19, 1863 - delivered the Gettysburg Address; November 8, 1864 - elected for second term as President; March 4, 1865 - inaugurated and delivered "With Malice Toward None" address; April 14, 1865 - shortly after 10 P.M. he was assassinated by John Wilkes Booth in Ford's Theatre, Washington, D.C.

Post-war achievements: Had successfully (after four bitter years of Civil War) maintained the Union

Date of death: April 15, 1865 at 7:22 A.M.

Place of burial: Springfield, Illinois

John Alexander Logan

Union

Date of birth: February 9, 1826

Birthplace: Jackson County, Illinois

U.S. Military Academy: no

Pre-war experience: lawyer, Mexican War service with Illinois volunteers, Illinois State Legislator, U.S. Congressman from Illinois, Democratic supporter of Stephen A. Douglas for President in 1860

Rank: Colonel - 31st Illinois, Brig. General, Major General

Major Battles and Campaigns: First Manassas (with Michigan regiment); Belmont, Fort Donelson - wounded (31st Illinois); "siege" of Corinth (Brigade); Vicksburg (Division, XVII Corps); Atlanta Campaign (XV Corps, temporarily commanded the Army of the Tennessee after the death of J.B. McPherson); "March to the Sea", Carolinas Campaign (XV Corps)

Post-war achievements: U.S. Congressman and Senator from Illinois, unsuccessful Republican nominee for Vice-President in 1884, helped organize the Grand Army of the Republic - served as president three times, writer

Date of death: December 26, 1886

Place of burial: Soldier's Home, Washington, D.C.

James Longstreet

Confederate

Date of birth: January 8, 1821

Birthplace: Edgefield District, South Carolina

U.S. Military Academy: Class of 1842 (54/62) Infantry

Pre-war experience: Mexican War - wounded, frontier and garrison duty, resigned from U.S. Army on June 1, 1861

Rank: Brig. General, Major General, Lt. General

Major Battles and Campaigns: First Manassas, (4th Brigade); Peninsular Campaign (Division); Second Manassas, Antietam (wing); Fredericksburg, Gettysburg (I Corps); Chickamauga, Knoxville (Ind. Corps command); Wilderness - wounded (Corps); defenses of Richmond, Appomattox (Corps)

Post-war achievements: president of insurance company, cotton factor, U.S. Minister to Turkey 1880, railroad commissioner, writer

Date of death: January 2, 1904

Place of burial: Gainesville, Georgia

William Wing Loring
Confederate

Date of birth: December 4, 1818

Birthplace: Wilmington, North Carolina

U.S. Military Academy: no

Pre-war experience: Seminole War, Georgetown College, lawyer, Florida legislator, commissioned into Regular Army in 1846, Mexican War - lost an arm at Chapultepec, frontier duty, Indian fighting, Utah Expedition, commanded Depts. of Oregon and New Mexico, youngest line colonel when he resigned from the U.S. Army on May 13, 1861

Rank: Brig. General, Major General

Major Battles and Campaigns: Romney Expedition; command in Southwestern Virginia; Vicksburg Campaign - cut off from Pemberton after Champion's Hill (Division); Atlanta Campaign; Franklin, Nashville (Corps); Carolinas Campaign, surrender of Johnston

Post-war achievements: New York banker, Egyptian military service 1869-1879, author

Date of death: December 30, 1886

Place of burial: St. Augustine, Florida

Eleanor S. Brockenbrough Library   Museum of the Confederacy

Nathaniel Lyon
Union

Date of birth: July 14, 1818

Birthplace: part of Ashford now Eastford, Connecticut

U.S. Military Academy: Class of 1841 (11/52) Infantry

Pre-war experience: Seminole and Mexican Wars, frontier duty in California and Kansas

Rank: Captain - 2nd U.S. Infantry, Brig. General

Major Battles and Campaigns: February 1861 - commander at St. Louis Arsenal; with help of Francis P. Blair the secessionists in eastern Missouri were neutralized and the encampment of the pro-southern Missouri militia at Camp Jackson in St. Louis was seized; Wilson's Creek - killed in action (commander)

Post-war achievements: North's first military hero

Date of death: August 10, 1861

Place of burial: Ashford, Connecticut

John Bankhead Magruder
Confederate

Date of birth: May 1, 1807

Birthplace: Port Royal, Virginia

U.S. Military Academy: Class of 1830 (15/42) Infantry

Pre-war experience: Seminole and Mexican Wars, garrison and frontier duty, resigned from U.S. Army on April 20, 1861

Rank: Colonel, Brig. General, Major General

Major Battles and Campaigns: Big Bethel, Peninsular Campaign, district and department commands in the Trans-Mississippi, Galveston, his troops opposed Bank's 1864 Red River Campaign, refused parole

Post-war achievements: Major General in Emperor Maximilian's Imperial forces in Mexico, lecturer

Date of death: February 18, 1871

Place of burial: Galveston, Texas

William Mahone
Confederate

Date of birth: December 1, 1826

Birthplace: Southampton County, Virginia

U.S. Military Academy: no

Pre-war experience: Virginia Military Institute 1847, teacher, railroad engineer, superintendent and president

Rank: Lt. Colonel - 6th Virginia, Colonel - same, Brig. General, Major General

Major Battles and Campaigns: capture of Norfolk Navy Yard; Peninsular Campaign, Second Manassas, Fredericksburg, Chancellorsville, Gettysburg, Wilderness, Spotsylvania, Cold Harbor, "Crater" at Petersburg (Brigade); took over command of Anderson's Division, Appomattox

Post-war achievements: President and creator of Norfolk Western R.R., U.S. Senator from Virginia, controlled politics in Virginia for a time

Date of death: October 8, 1895

Place of burial: Blandford Cemetery, Petersburg, Virginia

George Brinton McClellan
Union

Date of birth: December 3, 1826

Birthplace: Philadelphia, Pennsylvania

U.S. Military Academy: Class of 1846 (2/59) Engineers

Pre-war experience: attended University of Pennsylvania, Mexican War, instructor at West Point, translated and adapted French manual on bayonet exercise, engineering assignments at Fort Delaware and in the West, military commissioner to Europe during the Crimean War, adapted "McClellan" saddle, resigned from U.S. Army in 1857, railroad engineer and president

Rank: Major General, General-in-Chief

Major Battles and Campaigns: commanded Department of Ohio, Rich Mountain, commanded armies around Washington; Peninsular Campaign, Seven Days, Antietam (commanded the Army of the Potomac); from November 1862 he was "waiting orders" in New Jersey, resigned from U.S. Army on November 8, 1864

Post-war achievements: unsuccessful Democratic Presidential candidate in 1864, Chief Engineer of the New York City Department of Docks, Governor of New Jersey 1878-1881, writer

Date of death: October 29, 1885

Place of burial: Riverview Cemetery, Trenton, New Jersey

John Alexander McClernand
Union

Date of birth: May 30, 1812

Birthplace: near Hardinsburg, Kentucky

U.S. Military Academy: no

Pre-war experience: lawyer, Black Hawk War, Illinois State Legislator, U.S. Congressman from Illinois

Rank: Brig. General, Major General

Major Battles and Campaigns: Fort Henry, Shiloh (Division); Arkansas Post (commander); Vicksburg (XIII Corps); Red River Campaign 1864; resigned from U.S. Army on November 30, 1864

Post-war achievements: active in Democratic politics in Illinois

Date of death: September 20, 1890

Place of burial: Springfield, Illinois

Alexander McDowell McCook
Union

Date of birth: April 22, 1831

Birthplace: Columbiana County, Ohio

U.S. Military Academy: Class of 1852 (30/47) Infantry

Pre-war experience: frontier duty, instructor at West Point

Rank: Colonel - 1st Ohio Infantry, Brig. General, Major General

Major Battles and Campaigns: First Manassas (1st Ohio); Shiloh (2nd Division, Army of the Ohio); Corinth, Perryville (I Corps, Army of the Ohio); Stones River (Right Wing, XIV Corps, Army of the Cumberland); Chickamauga (XX Corps) - blamed, but exonerated for Union disaster, never again commanded field forces

Post-war achievements: served in the U.S. Army and advanced from Colonel to Major General, represented the United States at the coronation of Nicolas II of Russia 1896

Date of death: June 12, 1903

Place of burial: Cincinnati, Ohio

Ben McCulloch
Confederate

Date of birth: November 11, 1811

Birthplace: Rutherford County, Tennessee

U.S. Military Academy: no

Pre-war experience: followed Davy Crockett to Texas, Battle of San Jacinto, surveyor, Indian fighter, Texas Ranger, Mexican War, California "49-er", U.S. Marshall

Rank: Colonel - Texas State troops, Brig. General

Major Battles and Campaigns: Wilson's Creek (commander); Pea Ridge - killed in action (Brigade under Van Dorn)

Post-war achievements: none

Date of death: March 7, 1862

Place of burial: State Cemetery, Austin, Texas

41

Irvin McDowell

Union

Date of birth: October 15, 1818

Birthplace: Columbus, Ohio

U.S. Military Academy: Class of 1838 (23/45) Artillery

Pre-war experience: attended College de Troyes in France, instructor at West Point, Mexican War, frontier duty, staff duty in Washington

Rank: Brig. General, Major General

Major Battles and Campaigns: First Manassas (commander); Second Manassas (III Corps, Army of Virginia); witness at court-martial of Fitz John Porter; military board member and commissioner; commanded Department of the Pacific from July 1864

Post-war achievements: served in the U.S. Army in command of various Departments and Divisions

Date of death: May 4, 1885

Place of burial: Presidio, San Francisco, California

William McKinley

Union

Date of birth: January 29, 1843

Birthplace: Niles, Ohio

U.S. Military Academy: no

Pre-war experience: Allegheny College

Rank: Private, Comsy. Sgt., 2nd Lt., Capt., Brevet Major - 23rd Ohio

Major Battles and Campaigns: South Mountain, Antietam, Cloyd's Mountain, Shenandoah Valley Campaign -Winchester, Fisher's Hill, Cedar Creek

Post-war achievements: lawyer, U.S. House of Representatives 1877-1891, Governor of Ohio 1892-1896, elected 25th President of the United States 1896 and re-elected 1900, mortally wounded by an assassin in 1901

Date of death: September 14, 1901

Place of burial: Canton, Ohio

Lafayette McLaws
Confederate

Date of birth: January 15, 1821

Birthplace: Augusta, Georgia

U.S. Military Academy: Class of 1842 (48/56) Infantry

Pre-war experience: attended University of Virginia, Mexican War, frontier duty, Utah Expedition, resigned from U.S. Army on May 10, 1861

Rank: Major C.S.A., Colonel - 10th Georgia, Brig. General, Major General

Major Battles and Campaigns: Yorktown; Harpers Ferry, Antietam, Fredericksburg, Chancellorsville, Gettysburg, Chickamauga, Knoxville (Division); relieved by Longstreet after Fort Sanders debacle, but exonerated by President Davis; commanded District of Georgia; Carolinas Campaign, surrendered with J.E. Johnston

Post-war achievements: insurance businessman, collector of Internal Revenue, postmaster

Date of death: July 24, 1897

Place of burial: Savannah, Georgia

James Birdseye McPherson
Union

Date of birth: November 14, 1828

Birthplace: near Clyde, Ohio

U.S. Military Academy: Class of 1853 (1/52) Engineers

Pre-war experience: instructor at West Point, supervised harbor and river improvements and seacoast defenses on the Atlantic and Pacific coasts

Rank: 1st Lieutenant, Captain, Lt. Colonel, Colonel, Brig. General, Major General

Major Battles and Campaigns: staff assignment with Halleck; Chief Engineer with U.S. Grant at Forts Henry and Donelson, and Shiloh; Vicksburg (XVII Corps); Atlanta Campaign - killed in action (commanded Army of the Tennessee)

Post-war achievements: none

Date of death: July 22, 1864

Place of burial: Clyde, Ohio

George Gordon Meade
Union

Date of birth: December 31, 1815

Birthplace: Cadiz, Spain (American parents)

U.S. Military Academy: Class of 1835 (19/56) Artillery

Pre-war experience: served in Florida and on Ordnance duty at the Watertown (Mass.) Arsenal, resigned from the U.S. Army in 1836 to become a civil engineer, rejoined the Army in 1842 in the Corps of Topographical Engineers, Mexican War, engineered the construction of lighthouses and breakwaters and performed coastal and geodetic survey assignments

Rank: Brig. General, Major General

Major Battles and Campaigns: Peninsular Campaign - wounded twice, Second Manassas (Brigade); Antietam, Fredericksburg (Division, I Corps); Chancellorsville (V Corps); commanded the Army of the Potomac from Gettysburg, Wilderness, Spotsylvania, Cold Harbor, Petersburg to Appomattox (June 28, 1863 - June 27, 1865)

Post-war achievements: served in the U.S. Army in command of various Departments and Divisions

Date of death: November 6, 1872

Place of burial: Laurel Hill Cemetery, Philadelphia, Pennsylvania

Dixon Stansbury Miles
Union

Date of birth: ?? - ??, 1804

Birthplace: Baltimore County, Maryland

U.S. Military Academy: Class of 1824 (27/31) Infantry

Pre-war experience: Seminole and Mexican Wars, frontier and garrison duty

Rank: Colonel

Major Battles and Campaigns: First Manassas (5th Division - reserve); "waiting orders" from July 26, 1861, to March 8, 1862 - had been accused of drunkenness in battle by a Court of Inquiry, but there was no evidence to convict him; Harpers Ferry (commanded Harpers Ferry Railroad Brigade from March 1862 until he was mortally wounded during the Siege)

Post-war achievements: none

Date of death: September 16, 1862

Place of burial: Baltimore County, Maryland

George Washington Morgan
Union

Date of birth: September 20, 1820

Birthplace: Washington County, Pennsylvania

U.S. Military Academy: resigned in 1842 in his second year

Pre-war experience: Texas war of independence, lawyer, prosecutor of Knox County, Ohio, Mexican War - Colonel of 2nd Ohio and 15th U.S., discharged in 1848, farmer, U.S. Consul at Marseilles, Minister to Portugal

Rank: Brig. General

Major Battles and Campaigns: Cumberland Gap (7th Division, Army of the Ohio); Yazoo Expedition (3rd Division); Arkansas Post (XIII Corps); Vicksburg Campaign - resigned from U.S. Army on June 8, 1863, after disagreements with W.B. Sherman and the use of Negro troops

Post-war achievements: supporter of George B. McClellan for President in 1864, unsuccessfully ran for Governor of Ohio in 1865, U.S. Congressman from Ohio - opposed Radical Reconstruction

Date of death: July 26, 1893

Place of burial: Mount Vernon, Ohio

John Hunt Morgan
Confederate

Date of birth: June 1, 1825

Birthplace: Huntsville, Alabama

U.S. Military Academy: no

Pre-war experience: Transylvania College, enlisted in Mexican War, hemp manufacturer, general merchandise business, organized Lexington Rifles in 1857

Rank: Captain, Colonel - 2nd Kentucky Cavalry, Brig. General

Major Battles and Campaigns: Shiloh; numerous raids in Kentucky, Tennessee, Indiana, and Ohio, captured July 26, 1863, near New Lisbon, Ohio and imprisoned in Columbus. Escaped with others on November 26, 1863, and made his way south; from April 1864, he commanded the Department of Southwest Virginia; killed by Federal troops at Greeneville, Tennessee

Post-war achievements: none

Date of death: September 3, 1864

Place of burial: Lexington, Kentucky

John Singleton Mosby

Confederate

Date of birth: December 6, 1833

Birthplace: Edgemont, Virginia

U.S. Military Academy: no

Pre-war experience: attended University of Virginia, lawyer

Rank: Private - 1st Virginia Cavalry, 1st Lieutenant, Captain, Major, Lt. Colonel, Colonel

Major Battles and Campaigns: First Manassas, scout for JEB Stuart, organized Partisan Rangers in January 1863 (mustered into Confederate service on June 10, 1863, as the 43rd Battalion of Virginia Cavalry), conducted guerrilla warfare in northern Virginia, Rangers disbanded on April 20, 1865

Post-war achievements: lawyer, supporter of U.S. Grant, U.S. Consul in Hong Kong, writer

Date of death: May 30, 1916

Place of burial: Warrenton, Virginia

National Park Service   Fort Pulaski National Monument

Charles Hart Olmstead

Confederate

Date of birth: April 2, 1837

Birthplace: Savannah, Georgia

U.S. Military Academy: no

Pre-war experience: Georgia Military Institute 1856, clerk

Rank: Colonel - 1st Georgia Volunteers

Major Battles and Campaigns: Fort Pulaski (commander); Atlanta Campaign (Regiment)

Post-war achievements: lawyer, curator and Vice-President of the Georgia Historical Society, writer

Date of death: August 17, 1926

Place of burial: Savannah, Georgia

Edward Otho Cresap Ord
Union

Date of birth: October 18, 1818

Birthplace: Cumberland, Maryland

U.S. Military Academy: Class of 1839 (17/31) Artillery

Pre-war experience: Seminole War, in California during the Mexican War, Indian fighter in the Pacific Northwest, helped suppress John Brown at Harpers Ferry in 1859, garrison duty

Rank: Brig. General, Major General

Major Battles and Campaigns: Dranesville (Brigade, McCall's Division); Corinth - wounded (Division); Vicksburg (XIII Corps); Fort Harrison - wounded (XVIII Corps); Petersburg, Appomattox (XXIV Corps)

Post-war achievements: served in the U.S. Army in command of various Departments

Date of death: July 22, 1883

Place of burial: Arlington National Cemetery

John McCauley Palmer
Union

Date of birth: September 13, 1817

Birthplace: Scott County, Kentucky

U.S. Military Academy: no

Pre-war experience: attended Shurtleff College, lawyer, Illinois state senator, delegate to Republican convention nominating Lincoln, Washington Peace Conference delegate

Rank: Colonel - 14th Illinois, Brig. General, Major General

Major Battles and Campaigns: New Madrid, Island No. 10 (Division); Corinth (Brigade); Stones River, Chickamauga (Division); Chattanooga, Atlanta Campaign (XIV Corps)

Post-war achievements: Governor of Illinois 1868-1872, U.S. Senator, presidential candidate for Gold Democrats 1896

Date of death: September 25, 1900

Place of burial: Carlinville, Illinois

John Grubb Parke

Union

Date of birth: September 22, 1827

Birthplace: near Coatesville, Pennsylvania

U.S. Military Academy: Class of 1849 (2/43) Topographical Engineers

Pre-war experience: attended University of Pennsylvania, survey work with the Topographical Engineers and supervisor of river and harbor construction

Rank: 1st Lieutenant, Captain, Brig. General, Major General

Major Battles and Campaigns: Burnside's North Carolina Expedition (3rd Brigade); Antietam (3rd Division, IX Corps); Fredericksburg (Burnside's Chief of Staff); Vicksburg (IX Corps); Knoxville; Wilderness, Spotsylvania, James River Campaign (Burnside's Chief of Staff reporting directly to U.S. Grant); Petersburg (IX Corps); temporarily commanded the Army of the Potomac from December 30, 1864, to January 11, 1865, in Meade's absence

Post-war achievements: served in the U.S. Army with the Engineers, Assistant Chief of Engineers, Superintendent of West Point 1887-1889

Date of death: December 16, 1900

Place of burial: Philadelphia, Pennsylvania

Elisha Franklin "Bull" Paxton

Confederate

Date of birth: March 4, 1828

Birthplace: Rockbridge County, Virginia

U.S. Military Academy: no

Pre-war experience: Washington College, Yale University, University of Virginia law school, lawyer, farmer

Rank: 1st Lt. - Rockbridge Rifles, Major - 27th Virgnia, Brig. General

Major Battles and Campaigns: First Manassas; Shenandoah Valley Campaign, Seven Days, Second Manassas, Harpers Ferry, Antietam (Jackson's staff); Fredericksburg, Chancellorsville - killed in action (Brigade)

Post-war achievements: none

Date of death: May 3, 1863

Place of burial: Lexington, Virginia

John Pegram

Confederate

Date of birth: January 24, 1832

Birthplace: Petersburg, Virginia

U.S. Military Academy: Class of 1854 (10/46) Dragoons

Pre-war experience: frontier duty, instructor at West Point, Utah Expedition, resigned from U.S. Army on May 10, 1861

Rank: Lt. Colonel C.S.A., Colonel, Brig. General

Major Battles and Campaigns: Rich Mountain - captured; Chief Engineer for Beauregard and Bragg from April to October 1862; Lexington, Ky. (E.K. Smith's Chief of Staff); Stones River (Cavalry Brigade); Chickamauga (Division, Forrest's Corps); Wilderness - wounded (Brigade, Early's Division); Early's Shenandoah Valley Campaign (Brigade, succeeded to command of Rode's Division after the latter's death at Winchester); Petersburg - killed at Hatcher's Run

Post-war achievements: none

Date of death: February 6, 1865

Place of burial: Hollywood Cemetery, Richmond, Virginia

John Pelham

Confederate

Date of birth: September 14, 1838

Birthplace: near Alexandria, Alabama

U.S. Military Academy: resigned in May 1861 two weeks before graduation

Pre-war experience: student

Rank: Lieutenant, Captain, Major, Lt. Colonel - posthumously

Major Battles and Campaigns: First Manassas, Peninsular Campaign, Second Manassas, Antietam, Stuart's ride around McClellan, Fredericksburg, Kelly's Ford - killed in action (Artillery)

Post-war achievements: none

Date of death: March 17, 1863

Place of burial: Jacksonville, Alabama

John Clifford Pemberton
Confederate

Date of birth: August 10, 1814

Birthplace: Philadelphia, Pennsylvania

U.S. Military Academy: Class of 1837 (27/50) Artillery

Pre-war experience: Seminole and Mexican Wars, frontier duty, Utah Expedition, resigned from U.S. Army on April 24, 1861 and cast his lot with his wife's native Virginia

Rank: Lt. Colonel, Colonel, Brig. General, Major General, Lt.General

Major Battles and Campaigns: commanded Departments of South Carolina, Georgia and Florida, and Mississippi, Tennessee and East Louisiana; Vicksburg - surrendered July 4, 1863; resigned commission as General on May 18, 1864, after being exchanged, served as Lt. Colonel of Artillery by appointment of Jefferson Davis

Post-war achievements: farmer

Date of death: July 13, 1881

Place of burial: Philadelphia, Pennsylvania

William Dorsey Pender
Confederate

Date of birth: February 6, 1834

Birthplace: Edgecomb County, North Carolina

U.S. Military Academy: Class of 1854 (19/46) Artillery

Pre-war experience: frontier and garrison duty, resigned from U.S. Army on March 21, 1861

Rank: Captain - Artillery, Colonel - 3rd (later 13th) North Carolina and 6th North Carolina, Brig. General, Major General

Major Battles and Campaigns: Seven Pines (Colonel); Seven Days, Second Manassas, Fredericksburg, Chancellorsville - wounded three times (Brigade); Gettysburg - mortally wounded July 2, 1863 (Division, Hill's Corps)

Post-war achievements: none

Date of death: July 18, 1863, at Staunton, Virginia, after leg amputation

Place of burial: Tarboro, North Carolina

William Nelson Pendleton
Confederate

Date of birth: December 26, 1809

Birthplace: Richmond, Virginia

U.S. Military Academy: Class of 1830 (5/42) Artillery

Pre-war experience: garrison duty, instructor at West Point, resigned from U.S. Army in 1833, college teacher, Episcopal minister 1838

Rank: Captain - Rockbridge Artillery, Colonel, Brig. General

Major Battles and Campaigns: served as Chief of Artillery (perhaps nominally) of the Army of Northern Virginia from First Manassas through to Appomattox

Post-war achievements: Minister

Date of death: January 15, 1883

Place of burial: Lexington, Virginia

James Johnston Pettigrew
Confederate

Date of birth: July 4, 1828

Birthplace: Tyrrell County, North Carolina

U.S. Military Academy: no

Pre-war experience: University of North Carolina 1847, assistant professor at the Naval Observatory, lawyer, militia colonel

Rank: enlisted man - Hampton Legion, Colonel - 12th North Carolina, Brig. General

Major Battles and Campaigns: Fort Sumter; Peninsular Campaign - wounded and captured at Seven Pines; Gettysburg (Brigade, Heth's Division, succeeded to command of Division after Heth's wounding); Falling Waters, Maryland - mortally wounded July 14, 1863

Post-war achievements: none

Date of death: July 17, 1863

Place of burial: "Bonarva", Tyrrell County, North Carolina

Bill Turner

George Edward Pickett
Confederate

Date of birth: January 28, 1825

Birthplace: Richmond, Virginia

U.S. Military Academy: Class of 1846 (59/59) Infantry

Pre-war experience: Mexican War, frontier duty in Texas and in Washington Territory, resigned from U.S. Army on June 25, 1861

Rank: Colonel C.S.A., Brig. General, Major General

Major Battles and Campaigns: Peninsular Campaign - wounded at Gaines Mill (Brigade); Fredericksburg, Suffolk, Gettysburg (Division, Longstreet's Corps); New Bern (commanded Department of Virginia and North Carolina); Drewry's Bluff; Cold Harbor, Petersburg, Five Forks, Appomattox (Division, I Corps)

Post-war achievements: insurance businessman

Date of death: July 30, 1875

Place of burial: Richmond, Virginia

Albert Pike
Confederate

Date of birth: December 29, 1809

Birthplace: Boston, Massachusetts

U.S. Military Academy: no

Pre-war experience: attended Harvard, teacher, moved west, Mexican War veteran, poet, author, lawyer, editor, large property owner in Arkansas

Rank: Brig. General

Major Battles and Campaigns: Pea Ridge (commanded Department of Indian Territory); resigned from C.S. Army on July 12, 1862, but it was not accepted until November 5, 1862

Post-war achievements: lawyer, writer, Freemason

Date of death: April 2, 1891

Place of burial: Oak Hill Cemetery, Washington, D.C.

Gideon Johnson Pillow

Confederate

Date of birth: June 8, 1806

Birthplace: Williamson County, Tennessee

U.S. Military Academy: no

Pre-war experience: University of Nashville 1827, lawyer (partner of James K. Polk), Mexican War - wounded twice, politically active but unsuccessful

Rank: Senior Major General of the Provisional Army of Tennessee, Brig. General

Major Battles and Campaigns: Belmont; Fort Donelson (second-in-command, but fled with J.B. Floyd); reprimanded for his actions and held only minor posts for the remainder of the war

Post-war achievements: lawyer

Date of death: October 8, 1878

Place of burial: Memphis, Tennessee

Alfred Pleasonton

Union

Date of birth: July 7, 1824

Birthplace: Washington, D.C.

U.S. Military Academy: Class of 1844 (7/25) Dragoons

Pre-war experience: Mexican and Seminole Wars, frontier duty

Rank: Captain and Major - 2nd Dragoons (2nd U.S. Cavalry), Brig. General, Major General

Major Battles and Campaigns: Peninsular Campaign (Regiment); Antietam, Fredericksburg, Chancellorsville (Division, Cavalry Corps, Army of the Potomac); Brandy Station, Gettysburg (commanded Cavalry Corps, Army of the Potomac); Price's Missouri Raid October 1864 (commanded Department of Missouri)

Post-war achievements: served in the U.S. Army and in minor government posts, railroad president

Date of death: February 17, 1897

Place of burial: Congressional Cemetery, Washington, D.C.

Leonidas Polk

Confederate

Date of birth: April 10, 1806

Birthplace: Raleigh, North Carolina

U.S. Military Academy: Class of 1827 (8/38) Artillery

Pre-war experience: attended University of North Carolina, resigned from U.S. Army in 1828, Episcopal minister, Missionary Bishop of the Southwest, a founder of the University of the South

Rank: Major General, Lt. General

Major Battles and Campaigns: commanded Department No. 2 - defenses of the Mississippi River; Belmont, Shiloh, Perryville, Stones River, Chickamauga (Corps); Atlanta Campaign - killed in action at Pine Mountain, Georgia (Corps, Army of Tennessee)

Post-war achievements: none

Date of death: June 14, 1864

Place of burial: originally in Augusta, Georgia, re-interred in New Orleans, Louisiana in 1945

John Pope

Union

Date of birth: March 16, 1822

Birthplace: Louisville, Kentucky

U.S. Military Academy: Class of 1842 (17/56) Topographical Engineers

Pre-war experience: Mexican War, routine duty with the Topographical Engineers

Rank: Brig. General, Major General

Major Battles and Campaigns: New Madrid, Island No. 10, "siege" of Corinth (commanded the Army of the Mississippi); Second Manassas (commanded the Army of Virginia); commanded the Department of the Northwest - dealt with the Sioux uprising in Minnesota

Post-war achievements: served in the U.S. Army in various Department commands

Date of death: September 23, 1892

Place of burial: Bellefontaine Cemetery, St. Louis, Missouri

David Dixon Porter

Union

Date of birth: June 8, 1813

Birthplace: Chester, Pennsylvania

U.S. Military Academy: no

Pre-war experience: Midshipman U.S. Navy 1829, coastal survey, Mexican War, routine naval assignments

Rank: Commander, Rear Admiral

Major Battles and Campaigns: New Orleans (commanded mortar fleet under Farragut); Arkansas Post, Vicksburg, Red River Campaign 1864 (commanded Mississippi River Squadron); Fort Fisher (commanded North Atlantic Blockading Squadron)

Post-war achievements: served in the U.S. Navy, Superintendent of the Naval Academy, Annapolis, Maryland, writer

Date of death: February 13, 1891

Place of burial: Arlington National Cemetery

Fitz John Porter

Union

Date of birth: August 31, 1822

Birthplace: Portsmouth, New Hampshire

U.S. Military Academy: Class of 1845 (8/41) Artillery

Pre-war experience: Mexican War - wounded, instructor at West Point, Utah Expedition

Rank: Colonel - 15th U.S. Infantry, Brig. General, Major General

Major Battles and Campaigns: Peninsular Campaign (Division, III Corps); Seven Days (V Corps); Second Manassas (V Corps); Antietam - in reserve; victimized for his loyalty to McClellan, he was tried and dismissed from the Army on January 21, 1863, on charges brought up by Pope after Second Manassas

Post-war achievements: mine superintendent, merchant, New York City Commissioner of Police, Fire, and Public Works, exonerated of wartime charges in 1886

Date of death: May 21, 1901

Place of burial: Green-Wood Cemetery, Brooklyn, New York

Benjamin Mayberry Prentiss
Union

Date of birth: November 23, 1819

Birthplace: Belleville, Virginia (now West Virginia)

U.S. Military Academy: no

Pre-war experience: rope manufacturer, Illinois militia, lawyer

Rank: Captain and Colonel - 10th Illinois, Brig. General, Major General

Major Battles and Campaigns: Shiloh - captured at the "Hornet's Nest" (6th Division, Army of the Tennessee); Helena, Ark. July 1863 (commanded District of Eastern Arkansas); resigned from U.S. Army on October 28, 1863, because of poor health

Post-war achievements: lawyer, pension agent, postmaster of Bethany, Missouri

Date of death: February 8, 1901

Place of burial: Bethany, Missouri

Bill Turner

Sterling Price
Confederate

Date of birth: September 20, 1809

Birthplace: Prince Edward County, Virginia

U.S. Military Academy: no

Pre-war experience: Hampden-Sydney College, lawyer, farmer, Missouri State Legislator, U.S. Congressman from Missouri, Mexican War - Colonel of 2nd Missouri, Military Governor of New Mexico, Governor of Missouri 1853-1857

Rank: Major General

Major Battles and Campaigns: Wilson's Creek (with McCullough, commanded Missouri State Guard); Pea Ridge (under Van Dorn); Iuka, Corinth, Helena, Red River Campaign 1864; Missouri Raid 1864

Post-war achievements: none

Date of death: September 29, 1867

Place of burial: Bellefontaine Cemetery, St. Louis, Missouri

Civil War Library and Museum

Stephen Dodson Ramseur

Confederate

Date of birth: May 31, 1837

Birthplace: Lincolnton, North Carolina

U.S. Military Academy: Class of 1860 (14/41) Artillery

Pre-war experience: attended Davidson College, resigned from U.S. Army on April 6, 1861

Rank: Capt. - Ellis Light Art., Colonel - 49th N.C., Brig. General, Major General

Major Battles and Campaigns: Yorktown, Seven Days - severely wounded at Malvern Hill; Chancellorsville - wounded, Gettysburg, Wilderness, Spotsylvania - wounded (Brigade); Cold Harbor, Shenandoah Valley, Cedar Creek - mortally wounded on October 19, 1864 (Division)

Post-war achievements: none

Date of death: October 20, 1864

Place of burial: Lincolnton, North Carolina

John Fulton Reynolds

Union

Date of birth: September 20, 1820

Birthplace: Lancaster, Pennsylvania

U.S. Military Academy: Class of 1841 (26/52) Artillery

Pre-war experience: Mexican War, garrison and frontier duty, Utah Expedition, instructor and Commandant of Cadets at West Point

Rank: Lt. Colonel - 14th U.S. Infantry, Brig. General, Major General

Major Battles and Campaigns: Peninsular Campaign - captured after Glendale (Brigade, V Corps); Second Manassas (Division, III Corps); Fredericksburg, in reserve at Chancellorsville (I Corps); Gettysburg - killed in action (I Corps, Left Wing, Army of the Potomac)

Post-war achievements: none

Date of death: July 1, 1863

Place of burial: Lancaster, Pennsylvania

Israel Bush Richardson

Union

Date of birth: December 26, 1815

Birthplace: Fairfax, Vermont

U.S. Military Academy: Class of 1841 (38/52) Infantry

Pre-war experience: Seminole and Mexican Wars, frontier duty, resigned from U.S. Army in 1855 to farm in Pontiac, Michigan

Rank: Colonel - 2nd Michigan Infantry, Brig. General

Major Battles and Campaigns: First Manassas (4th Brigade, 1st Division); Peninsular Campaign (Division, II Corps); Antietam - mortally wounded September 17, 1862 (Division, I Corps)

Post-war achievements: none

Date of death: November 3, 1862

Place of burial: Pontiac, Michigan

James Brewerton Ricketts

Union

Date of birth: June 21, 1817

Birthplace: New York City, New York

U.S. Military Academy: Class of 1839 (16/31) Artillery

Pre-war experience: Mexican and Seminole Wars, garrison duty

Rank: Captain - 1st U.S. Artillery, Brig. General

Major Battles and Campaigns: First Manassas - wounded four times and captured (Battery); Cedar Mountain, Second Manassas (Division, III Corps, Army of Virginia); Antietam - wounded (Division, I Corps); commissions and courts-martial until April 1864; Wilderness, Spotsylvania, North Anna, Cold Harbor, Petersburg, Early's Washington Raid, Shenandoah Valley - wounded at Cedar Creek (Division, VI Corps)

Post-war achievements: served briefly in the U.S. Army until he retired for disabilities from battle wounds

Date of death: September 22, 1887

Place of burial: Arlington National Cemetery

Robert Emmett Rodes
Confederate

Date of birth: March 29, 1829

Birthplace: Lynchburg, Virginia

U.S. Military Academy: no

Pre-war experience: Virginia Military Institute 1848, instructor at V.M.I., civil engineer

Rank: Colonel - 5th Alabama, Brig. General, Major General

Major Battles and Campaigns: First Manassas (5th Alabama); Peninsular Campaign - wounded at Seven Pines (Brigade); Antietam - wounded, Fredericksburg, Chancellorsville (Brigade); Gettysburg, Wilderness, Spotsylvania (Division); Early's Shenandoah Valley Campaign - killed in action at Winchester

Post-war achievements: none

Date of death: September 19, 1864

Place of burial: Lynchburg, Virginia

William Starke Rosecrans
Union

Date of birth: September 6, 1819

Birthplace: Delaware County, Ohio

U.S. Military Academy: Class of 1842 (5/56) Engineers

Pre-war experience: routine engineering assignments, instructor at West Point, resigned from U.S. Army in 1854, civil engineer, architect, kerosene refiner

Rank: Colonel - 23rd Ohio, Brig. General, Major General

Major Battles and Campaigns: Rich Mountain (Brigade); Carnifex Ferry (Army of Occupation); Iuka, Corinth; Stones River, Tullahoma Campaign, Chickamauga (commanded the Army of the Cumberland); after the latter defeat he "awaited orders" and commanded the Department of Missouri

Post-war achievements: resigned from U.S. Army in 1867, Minister to Mexico, U.S. Congressman from California, Register of the Treasury, rancher

Date of death: March 11, 1898

Place of burial: originally in Los Angeles, California, re-interred in Arlington National Cemetery in 1902

Thomas Lafayette Rosser
Confederate

Date of birth: October 15, 1836

Birthplace: Campbell County, Virginia

U.S. Military Academy: Class of 1861, resigned two weeks before graduation

Pre-war experience: student

Rank: 1st Lt. & Capt. - Washington Art. of New Orleans, Colonel - 5th Va. Cav., Brig. General, Major General

Major Battles and Campaigns: First Manassas, Peninsula Campaign - wounded at Mechanicsville (Wash. Art.); Catlett's Station, Second Manassas, South Mountain, Kelly's Ford - wounded, Chancellorsville, Gettysburg (5th Va. Cav.); Buckland Mills, Wilderness, Spotsylvania, Trevilian Station (Brigade); Shenandoah Valley, Woodstock, Cedar Creek, independent raids, Petersburg, Five Forks, Appomattox

Post-war achievements: chief engineer of the Northern Pacific and Canadian Pacific Railroads, gentleman farmer, appointed Brig. General of U.S. Volunteers during Spanish-American War 1898

Date of death: March 29, 1910

Place of burial: Riverview Cemetery, Charlottesville, Virginia

John McAllister Schofield
Union

Date of birth: September 29, 1831

Birthplace: Gerry, New York

U.S. Military Academy: Class of 1853 (7/52) Artillery

Pre-war experience: served in U.S. Army in Florida, instructor at West Point, under a leave of absence in 1860 he taught at Washington University in St. Louis

Rank: Captain - 1st U.S. Artillery, Major - 1st Missouri Infantry (reorganized as Artillery), Brig. General, Major General

Major Battles and Campaigns: Wilson's Creek (Lyon's Chief of Staff); commanded various occupational troops in Tennessee and Missouri; Atlanta Campaign, Franklin, Nashville (XXIII Corps); operations in North Carolina and surrender of J.E. Johnston (commanded Department of North Carolina)

Post-war achievements: Secretary of War under Johnson while serving in the U.S. Army, recommended Pearl Harbor as a naval base, Superintendent of West Point, Commander-in-Chief of the Army 1888-1895

Date of death: March 4, 1906

Place of burial: Arlington National Cemetery

Winfield Scott
Union

Date of birth: June 13, 1786

Birthplace: near Petersburg, Virginia

U.S. Military Academy: no

Pre-war experience: attended William and Mary, War of 1812 - wounded, Mexican War, Commander-in-Chief of the Army 1841-1861, unsuccessful candidate for President in 1852

Rank: Lieutenant General

Major Battles and Campaigns: devised the "Anaconda Plan", retired from the U.S. Army on October 31, 1861

Post-war achievements: writer, travelled abroad

Date of death: May 29, 1866

Place of burial: West Point, New York

John Sedgwick
Union

Date of birth: September 13, 1813

Birthplace: Cornwall Hollow, Connecticut

U.S. Military Academy: Class of 1837 (24/50) Artillery

Pre-war experience: Seminole and Mexican Wars, garrison and frontier duty, Utah Expedition

Rank: Colonel - 1st U.S. Cavalry, Brig. General, Major General

Major Battles and Campaigns: Peninsular Campaign - wounded at Glendale, Antietam - wounded three times (Division, II Corps); Marye's Heights, Salem Church, Gettysburg (VI Corps); Rappahannock Bridge (V and VI Corps); Wilderness, Spotsylvania - killed in action (VI Corps)

Post-war achievements: none

Date of death: May 9, 1864

Place of burial: Cornwall Hollow, Connecticut

Philip Henry Sheridan

Union

Date of birth: March 6, 1831

Birthplace: Albany, New York

U.S. Military Academy: Class of 1853 (34/52) Infantry-Cavalry

Pre-war experience: frontier duty in the U.S. Army

Rank: Captain, Colonel - 2nd Michigan Cavalry, Brig. General, Major General

Major Battles and Campaigns: Perryville (11th Division, Army of the Ohio); Stones River (3rd Division, XVI Corps); Chickamauga (3rd Division, XX Corps); Chattanooga (Division, IV Corps); Wilderness, Spotsylvania, Yellow Tavern, Trevilian Raid (Cavalry Corps, Army of the Potomac); Shenandoah Valley Campaign - Winchester, Fishers Hill, Cedar Creek, Waynesboro (commanded the Middle Military Division - VI and XIX Corps and three divisions of cavalry); Five Forks, Appomattox Campaign

Post-war achievements: served in the U.S. Army in command of various Districts, Departments and Divisions, Commander-in-Chief of the Army 1884-1888, writer

Date of death: August 5, 1888

Place of burial: Arlington National Cemetery

William Tecumseh Sherman

Union

Date of birth: February 8, 1820

Birthplace: Lancaster, Ohio

U.S. Military Academy: Class of 1840 (6/42) Artillery

Pre-war experience: routine frontier and garrison duty, resigned from U.S. Army in 1853, banker, lawyer, school superintendent

Rank: Colonel - 13th U.S. Infantry, Brig. General, Major General

Major Battles and Campaigns: First Manassas (3rd Brigade); Shiloh - wounded (5th Division, Army of the Tennessee); Chickasaw Bluffs, Arkansas Post; Vicksburg (XV Corps); Chattanooga (Department of the Tennessee); Atlanta Campaign, "March to the Sea", Carolinas Campaign, surrender of J.E. Johnston (Military Division of the Mississippi)

Post-war achievements: Commander-in-Chief of the Army 1869-1883, speaker

Date of death: February 14, 1891

Place of burial: Calvary Cemetery, St. Louis, Missouri

Daniel Edgar Sickles
Union

Date of birth: October 20, 1819

Birthplace: New York City, New York

U.S. Military Academy: no

Pre-war experience: attended New York University, lawyer, New York State Senator, U.S. Congressman from New York 1857-1861

Rank: Colonel - 20th New York, Brig. General, Major General

Major Battles and Campaigns: Peninsular Campaign (Brigade, III Corps); Antietam, Fredericksburg (2nd Division, III Corps); Chancellorsville, Gettysburg - wounded on July 2, 1863, and lost right leg (III Corps)

Post-war achievements: Military Governor of South Carolina, U.S. Minister to Spain, U.S. Congressman from New York, Chairman of the New York State Monuments Commission - worked to establish the Gettysburg battlefield as a National Military Park

Date of death: May 3, 1914

Place of burial: Arlington National Cemetery

Adam Jacoby Slemmer
Union

Date of birth: January 24, 1829

Birthplace: Montgomery County, Pennsylvania

U.S. Military Academy: Class of 1850 (12/44) Artillery

Pre-war experience: Seminole War, frontier duty, instructor at West Point

Rank: 1st Lieutenant - 1st U.S. Artillery, Major - 16th U.S. Infantry, Brig. General

Major Battles and Campaigns: Fort Pickens - prevented seizure by the state of Florida from January - April 1861; Stones River - severely wounded on December 31, 1862 (portion of 16th U.S., Rousseau's Division, XIV Corps); staff and board duty with the Army in Ohio

Post-war achievements: garrison duty in the U.S. Army

Date of death: October 7, 1868

Place of burial: Norristown, Pennsylvania

Henry Warner Slocum

Union

Date of birth: September 24, 1827

Birthplace: Delphi, New York

U.S. Military Academy: Class of 1852 (7/43) Artillery

Pre-war experience: served in Florida and South Carolina, resigned from the U.S. Army in 1856, lawyer, New York State Legislator, Colonel - New York State militia

Rank: Colonel - 27th New York, Brig. General, Major General

Major Battles and Campaigns: First Manassas - wounded (27th N.Y.); Yorktown (Brigade); Seven Days, Second Manassas, Antietam (Division, VI Corps); Chancellorsville, Gettysburg (XII Corps); capture of Atlanta (XX Corps); "March to the Sea", Carolinas Campaign, surrender of J.E. Johnston (commanded XIV and XX Corps designated the Army of Georgia)

Post-war achievements: resigned from U.S. Army in September 1865, lawyer, U.S. Congressman from New York (three terms), served on Board of Gettysburg Monument Commissioners

Date of death: April 14, 1894

Place of burial: Green-Wood Cemetery, Brooklyn, New York

Edmund Kirby Smith

Confederate

Date of birth: May 16, 1824

Birthplace: St. Augustine, Florida

U.S. Military Academy: Class of 1845 (25/41) Infantry

Pre-war experience: Mexican War, instructor at West Point, garrison and frontier duty, resigned from U.S. Army on March 3, 1861

Rank: Colonel C.S.A. Cavalry, Brig. General, Major General, Lt. General, Full General

Major Battles and Campaigns: First Manassas - severely wounded (4th Brigade); Richmond, Perryville (commanded Department of East Tennessee); Red River Campaign 1864, Arkansas Campaign (commanded Trans-Mississippi Department); surrendered on June 2, 1865 to E.R.S. Canby at Galveston, Texas

Post-war achievements: president of telegraph company, college professor and president

Date of death: March 28, 1893

Place of burial: Sewanee, Tennessee

Martin Luther Smith
Confederate

Date of birth: September 9, 1819

Birthplace: Danby, Tompkins County, New York

U.S. Military Academy: Class of 1842 (16/56) Topographical Engineers

Pre-war experience: Mexican War, surveying in Florida, Georgia and Texas, resigned from the U.S. Army on April 1, 1861

Rank: Major - Corps of Engineers, Colonel - 21st La., Brig. General, Major General

Major Battles and Campaigns: planned and built fortifications at New Orleans and Vicksburg; Vicksburg (Division) - unexchanged for seven months after capture; chief engineer of Army of Northern Virginia, Army of Tennessee and at Mobile, Alabama

Post-war achievements: civil engineer

Date of death: July 29, 1866

Place of burial: Athens, Georgia

Carter Littlepage Stevenson
Confederate

Date of birth: September 21, 1817

Birthplace: Fredericksburg, Virginia

U.S. Military Academy: Class of 1838 (42/45) Infantry

Pre-war experience: Frontier duty, Mexican War, Indian fighting, Utah Expedition, resigned from U.S. Army on June 6, 1861 but document was not forwarded to War Dept. - therefore he was dismissed on June 25, 1861

Rank: Major - Inf., Colonel - 53rd Virginia, Brig. General, Major General

Major Battles and Campaigns: Cumberland Gap, Richmond, Perryville; Vicksburg Campaign - captured (Division); Missionary Ridge, Atlanta Campaign, Nashville, Carolinas Campaign, Bentonville, surrender of Johnston

Post-war achievements: civil and mining engineer

Date of death: August 15, 1888

Place of burial: Fredericksburg, Virginia

Alexander Peter Stewart
Confederate

Date of birth: October 2, 1821

Birthplace: Rogersville, Tennessee

U.S. Military Academy: Class of 1842 (12/56) Artillery

Pre-war experience: garrison duty, instructor at West Point, resigned from U.S. Army in 1845, professor at Cumberland Univ. and Univ. of Nashville

Rank: Major - Art., Brig. General, Major General, Lt. General

Major Battles and Campaigns: Columbus, KY and Belmont, MO (heavy art.); Shiloh, Perryville, Stones River (Brigade); Chickamauga, Chattanooga, Atlanta Campaign - wounded at Ezra Church (Division); Franklin, Nashville, Carolinas Campaign (Corps), surrender of Johnston

Post-war achievements: professor, insurance business in St. Louis, chancellor of Univ. of Miss. 1874-1886, park commissioner of Chickamauga & Chattanooga Natl. Mil. Park

Date of death: August 30, 1908

Place of burial: St. Louis, Missouri

Eleanor S. Brockenbrough Library   Museum of the Confederacy

James Ewell Brown Stuart
Confederate

Date of birth: February 6, 1833

Birthplace: Patrick County, Virginia

U.S. Military Academy: Class of 1854 (13/46) Mounted Rifles-Cavalry

Pre-war experience: frontier duty, aide to R.E. Lee at capture of John Brown at Harpers Ferry in 1859, resigned from U.S. Army on May 3, 1861

Rank: Colonel - 1st Virginia Cavalry, Brig. General, Major General

Major Battles and Campaigns: First Manassas, Dranesville; Peninsular Campaign, "Ride around McClellan", Seven Days; Second Manassas, Antietam, Fredericksburg, Chancellorsville - temporarily commanded Jackson's Corps, Brandy Station, Gettysburg, Wilderness, Spotsylvania, Yellow Tavern - mortally wounded May 11, 1864 (Cavalry Division, Army of Northern Virginia)

Post-war achievements: none

Date of death: May 12, 1864

Place of burial: Hollywood Cemetery, Richmond, Virginia

Edwin Vose Sumner
Union

Date of birth: January 30, 1797

Birthplace: Boston, Massachusetts

U.S. Military Academy: no

Pre-war experience: commissioned 2nd Lt. in 1819, Black Hawk War, Mexican War (wounded), frontier duty, Kansas disturbances

Rank: Brig. General, Major General

Major Battles and Campaigns: Peninsula Campaign - wounded twice, South Mountain, Antietam (II Corps); Fredericksburg (Right Grand Division - II & IX Corps)

Post-war achievements: none, died of natural causes; the oldest active corps commander in the Civil War

Date of death: March 21, 1863

Place of burial: Oakwood Cemetery, Syracuse, New York

George Sykes
Union

Date of birth: October 9, 1822

Birthplace: Dover, Delaware

U.S. Military Academy: Class of 1842 (39/56) Infantry

Pre-war experience: Seminole and Mexican Wars, frontier duty and Indian fighting

Rank: Captain, Major - 14th U.S. Infantry, Brig. General, Major General

Major Battles and Campaigns: First Manassas (Battalion of Regulars); Peninsular Campaign (Brigade of Regulars); Seven Days, Second Manassas (Division, V Corps); in reserve at Antietam and Fredericksburg; Chancellorsville (Division, V Corps); Gettysburg, Mine Run Campaign (V Corps - relieved in December 1863); Department of Kansas

Post-war achievements: served in the U.S. Army on garrison duty until his death

Date of death: February 8, 1880

Place of burial: West Point, New York

George Henry Thomas

Union

Date of birth: July 31, 1816

Birthplace: Southampton County, Virginia

U.S. Military Academy: Class of 1840 (12/42) Artillery

Pre-war experience: garrison duty, Seminole and Mexican Wars, instructor at West Point, Indian fighting

Rank: Colonel - 2nd U.S. Cavalry, Brig. General, Major General

Major Battles and Campaigns: Mill Springs, Ky., Shiloh, Corinth (1st Division, Army of the Ohio); Perryville (second in command); Stones River (Centre Division, XIV Corps); Tullahoma Campaign, Chickamauga (XIV Corps); Chattanooga, Atlanta Campaign, Franklin, Nashville (commanded Army and Department of the Cumberland)

Post-war achievements: served in the U.S. Army until his death

Date of death: March 28, 1870

Place of burial: Oakwood Cemetery, Troy, New York

Library of Congress

Isaac Ridgeway Trimble

Confederate

Date of birth: May 15, 1802

Birthplace: Culpeper County, Virginia

U.S. Military Academy: Class of 1822 (17/40) Artillery

Pre-war experience: ordnance and topographical engineering duty, resigned from U.S. Army in 1832, railroad engineer and superintendent

Rank: Colonel of Engineers C.S.A., Brig. General, Major General

Major Battles and Campaigns: Jackson's Shenandoah Valley Campaign, Seven Days, Cedar Mountain, Second Manassas - severely wounded (Brigade); Gettysburg - wounded and captured on July 3, 1863, in "Pickett's Charge" (commanded Pender's Division); not exchanged until February 1865

Post-war achievements: consulting engineer

Date of death: January 2, 1888

Place of burial: Green Mount Cemetery, Baltimore, Maryland

Emory Upton
Union

Date of birth: August 27, 1839

Birthplace: Batavia, New York

U.S. Military Academy: Class of May, 1861 (8/45) Artillery

Pre-war experience: attended Oberlin College, Ohio

Rank: 2nd Lt. - 4th U.S. Art., 1st Lt. - 5th U.S. Art., Colonel - 121st N.Y., Brig. General

Major Battles and Campaigns: First Manassas - wounded (Gen. Tyler's A.D.C.); Yorktown, West Point, Gaines's Mill, Glendale (Battery); South Mountain, Antietam (Art. Brigade); Fredericksburg, Salem Church, Gettysburg, Mine Run, Wilderness, Spotsylvania - wounded (121st N.Y.); Cold Harbor, Petersburg, Shenandoah Valley Campaign - wounded at Opequon (Brigade/Division); Wilson's Raid, Selma (4th Cav. Division)

Post-war achievements: regular army service with 25th U.S. Infantry, commandant of cadets at West Point 1870-1875, author of numerous military treatises, commander of the Presidio in San Francisco - committed suicide

Date of death: March 15, 1881

Place of burial: Fort Hill Cemetery, Auburn, New York

Earl Van Dorn
Confederate

Date of birth: September 17, 1820

Birthplace: near Port Gibson, Mississippi

U.S. Military Academy: Class of 1842 (52/56) Infantry

Pre-war experience: Mexican and Seminole Wars, frontier duty, Indian fighting, resigned from U.S. Army on January 31, 1861

Rank: Colonel, Brig. General, Major General

Major Battles and Campaigns: Pea Ridge (commanded Army of the West); Corinth (Army of Mississippi); Holly Springs, Thompson's Station (Cavalry); assassinated at Spring Hill, Tennessee

Post-war achievements: none

Date of death: May 7, 1863

Place of burial: Port Gibson, Mississippi

Lewis Wallace

Union

Date of birth: April 10, 1827

Birthplace: Brookville, Indiana

U.S. Military Academy: no

Pre-war experience: reporter, lawyer, Mexican War - 1st Indiana, Indiana State Senator, Indiana militia officer

Rank: Colonel - 11th Indiana, Brig. General, Major General

Major Battles and Campaigns: Romney (11th Indiana); Fort Donelson (3rd Division under Grant); Shiloh (3rd Division, Army of the Tennessee); member of various boards and commissions; Monocacy, Md. (VIII Corps)

Post-war achievements: served on the Commission that tried the Lincoln conspirators, President of the court-martial that tried and sentenced Henry Wirz, Governor of New Mexico Territory, U.S. Minister to Turkey, author, speaker

Date of death: February 15, 1905

Place of burial: Oak Hill Cemetery, Crawfordsville, Indiana

Library of Congress

William Henry Talbot Walker

Confederate

Date of birth: November 26, 1816

Birthplace: Augusta, Georgia

U.S. Military Academy: Class of 1837 (46/50) Infantry

Pre-war experience: Seminole War - 3 wounds, resigned from Army in 1838 but reappointed in 1840, Mexican War - gravely wounded, commandant of cadets at West Point, frontier duty, resigned from U.S. Army on December 20, 1860

Rank: Brig. General, Major General

Major Battles and Campaigns: Pensacola (Brigade); Vicksburg Campaign with Johnston (Brigade); Chickamauga (Reserve Corps), Atlanta Campaign - killed in action at Battle of Atlanta (Division)

Post-war achievements: none

Date of death: July 22, 1864

Place of burial: Augusta, Georgia

Gouverneur Kemble Warren
Union

Date of birth: January 8, 1830

Birthplace: Cold Spring, New York

U.S. Military Academy: Class of 1850 (2/44) Topographical Engineers

Pre-war experience: topographical engineering assignments, instructor at West Point, frontier duty

Rank: Lt. Colonel - 5th New York Infantry, Colonel - same, Brig. General, Major General

Major Battles and Campaigns: Big Bethel, Peninsular Campaign (5th N.Y.); Seven Days - wounded, Second Manassas, in reserve at Antietam and Fredericksburg (Brigade, V Corps); Gettysburg - wounded (Chief Engineer, Army of the Potomac); Bristoe Station, Kelly's Ford, Mine Run (II Corps); Wilderness, Spotsylvania, North Anna, Cold Harbor, Petersburg, Five Forks (V Corps); relieved by Sheridan at Five Forks for dilatory leadership

Post-war achievements: served in the U.S. Army Corps of Engineers, writer, exonerated for Five Forks in 1879, but the findings were not published until just before Warren's death

Date of death: August 8, 1882

Place of burial: Island Cemetery, Newport, Rhode Island

Joseph Wheeler
Confederate

Date of birth: September 10, 1836

Birthplace: Augusta, Georgia

U.S. Military Academy: Class of 1859 (19/22) Dragoons-Mounted Rifles

Pre-war experience: frontier duty, resigned from the U.S. Army on April 22, 1861

Rank: 1st Lieutenant, Colonel - 19th Alabama, Brig. General, Major General

Major Battles and Campaigns: Shiloh (19th Alabama); numerous cavalry raids, Perryville, Stones River, Knoxville, Chattanooga, Atlanta Campaign, "March to the Sea", Carolinas Campaign (commanded the Cavalry of the Army of Tennessee from July 1862 until replaced by W. Hampton during the Carolinas Campaign), captured in May 1865

Post-war achievements: merchant, U.S. Congressman from Alabama (elected eight times), Major General of U.S. Volunteers in Spanish-American War, writer

Date of death: January 25, 1906

Place of burial: Arlington National Cemetery

James Harrison Wilson

Union

Date of birth: September 2, 1837

Birthplace: near Shawneetown, Illinois

U.S. Military Academy: Class of 1860 (6/41) Topographical Engineers

Pre-war experience: topographical engineer in the Department of Oregon

Rank: 1st Lieutenant, Lt. Colonel, Brig. General, Major General

Major Battles and Campaigns: Port Royal Expedition, Fort Pulaski, Antietam, Vicksburg, Chattanooga, Knoxville (Engineering staff for Sherman, Hunter, McClellan and Grant); Wilderness, Spotsylvania, Yellow Tavern, Petersburg, Shenandoah Valley (Cavalry Division under Sheridan); Franklin, Nashville, Wilson's Raid (Chief of Cavalry, Military Division of the Mississippi)

Post-war achievements: served in the U.S. Army until 1870, railroad construction, writer, Major General of U.S. Volunteers in Spanish-American War, Boxer Rebellion, represented the U.S. at the coronation of Edward VII of England

Date of death: February 23, 1925

Place of burial: Wilmington, Delaware

The execution of Henry Wirz: Wirz has his back to the railing to the right of the steps.

Heinrich (Henry) Hartmann Wirz

Confederate

Date of birth: November 25, 1823

Birthplace: Zurich, Switzerland

U.S. Military Academy: no

Pre-war experience: mercantile business with father in Switzerland, immigrated to the United States in 1849, factory worker in Massachusetts, medical assistant in Kentucky and Louisiana

Rank: Private and Sergeant - 4th Louisiana, Captain, Major

Major Battles and Campaigns: Seven Pines - wounded (4th Louisiana); prison official in Richmond and performed assignments for J.H. Winder; envoy to Paris and Berlin; ordered to Andersonville Prison on March 27, 1864, and assumed command of the interior of the prison

Post-war achievements: arrested May 7, 1865, tried by a Military Commission and found guilty of excessive cruelty to Federal prisoners and condemned to death. "The sole execution because of the War."

Date of death: November 12, 1865, by hanging

Place of burial: originally beside the body of Lincoln conspirator Atzerodt on the Washington Arsenal grounds, his body was removed to Olivet Cemetery